Edwin Vanderbruggen

Reconstructing Global Tax Governance

The Proposed UN Framework Convention on International Tax Cooperation

Springer

Edwin Vanderbruggen
Faculty of Law
Foreign Trade University
Ha Noi, Vietnam

ISSN 2192-855X ISSN 2192-8568 (electronic)
SpringerBriefs in Law
ISBN 978-981-95-5616-8 ISBN 978-981-95-5617-5 (eBook)
https://doi.org/10.1007/978-981-95-5617-5

This Springer imprint is published by the registered company Springer Nature Singapore Pte Ltd.
The registered company address is: 152 Beach Road, #21-01/04 Gateway East, Singapore 189721, Singapore

SpringerBriefs in Law

SpringerBriefs present concise summaries of cutting-edge research and practical applications across a wide spectrum of fields. Featuring compact volumes of 50 to 125 pages, the series covers a range of content from professional to academic. Typical topics might include:

- A timely report of state-of-the art analytical techniques
- A bridge between new research results, as published in journal articles, and a contextual literature review
- A snapshot of a hot or emerging topic
- A presentation of core concepts that students must understand in order to make independent contributions

SpringerBriefs in Law showcase emerging theory, empirical research, and practical application in Law from a global author community. SpringerBriefs are characterized by fast, global electronic dissemination, standard publishing contracts, standardized manuscript preparation and formatting guidelines, and expedited production schedules.

Competing Interests The author has no competing interests to declare that are relevant to the content of this manuscript.

Abbreviations

ACCTS	Agreement on Climate Change, Trade and Sustainability
Ad Hoc Committee	Ad Hoc Committee to Draft Terms of Reference for a United Nations Framework Convention on International Tax Cooperation
AEOI	Automatic Exchange of Information
AO	Advisory Opinion
APAs	Advance Pricing Arrangements
BEPS	Base Erosion and Profit Shifting
CARF	Crypto-Asset Reporting Framework
CbC Reporting	Country-by-Country Reporting
CBDR-RC	Common but Differentiated Responsibilities and Respective Capabilities
CEDAW	Committee on the Elimination of Discrimination against Women
CERD	Committee on the Elimination of Racial Discrimination
CESCR	Committee on Economic, Social and Cultural Rights
CJEU	Court of Justice of the European Union
COP	Conference of the Parties
CoRA	Comparative Risk Assessment
CORSIA	Carbon Offsetting and Reduction Scheme for International Aviation
CPTPP	Comprehensive and Progressive Agreement for Trans-Pacific Partnership
DMTT	Domestic Minimum Top-up Tax
DRM	Domestic Resource (Revenue) Mobilization
DSTs	Digital Service Taxes
DTA	Double Taxation Agreement
ECtHR	European Court of Human Rights
EOIR	Exchange of Information on Request
ETR	Effective Tax Rate

EU	European Union
FCTC	Framework Convention on Tobacco Control
FTA	Forum on Tax Administration
FTA	Free Trade Agreement
FTC	UN Framework Convention on International Tax Cooperation
G20	Group of 20
GHG	Greenhouse Gas
Global Forum	Global Forum on Transparency and Exchange of Information for Tax Purposes
GLITI	Global Intangible Low-Taxed Income
GLoBE	Global Anti-base Erosion Rules
HICs	High-Income Countries
IACtHR	Inter-American Court of Human Right
ICAO	International Civil Aviation Organization
ICAP	International Compliance Assurance Programme
ICCPR	International Covenant on Civil and Political Rights
ICESCR	International Covenant on Economic, Social and Cultural Rights
ICJ	International Court of Justice
IF	Inclusive Framework
IFF	Illicit Financial Flows
IIR	Income Inclusion Rule
ILA	International Law Association
IMF	International Monetary Fund
IMO	International Maritime Organization
INC	Intergovernmental Negotiating Committee
ISDS	Investor-State Dispute Settlement
ITLOS	International Tribunal for the Law of the Sea
LMICs	Low- and Middle-Income Countries
MAAC	Mutual Administrative Assistance in Tax Matters
MAP	Mutual Agreement Procedures
Members	Member States
MLC	Multilateral Convention
MLI	Multilateral Instrument
MNEs	Multinational Enterprises
MPIA	Multi-Party Interim Appeal Arbitration Arrangement
OECD	Organisation for Economic Co-operation and Development
PCA	Permanent Court of Arbitration
PCIJ	Permanent Court of Justice
Pillar 1 (G20/OECD/ IF)	Global Digital Economy
Pillar 2 (BEPS)	Global Minimum Tax
QDMTT	Qualified Domestic Minimum Top-up Tax
RCEP	Regional Comprehensive Economic Partnership

RIAA	Reports of International Arbitral Awards
RTP	Responsible Tax Principles
SDGs	Sustainable Development Goals
STTR	Subject to Tax Rule
SG Report	Secretary-General Report on 'Promotion of inclusive and effective international tax cooperation at the United Nations' dated 26 July 2023
TIEAs	Tax Information Exchange Agreements
TIWB	Tax Inspectors without Borders
TOR	Terms of Reference
TPG	Transfer Pricing Guidelines
TREAT	Tax Risk Evaluation and Assurance Tool
UNFCCC	United Nations Framework Convention on Climate Change
UNFCITC	United Nations Framework Convention on International Tax Cooperation
UNGA	United Nations General Assembly
UN Tax Committee	United Nations Committee of Experts on International Cooperation in Tax Matters
UNTS	United Nations Treaty Series
UTPR	Undertaxed Payments Rule
VAT	Value Added Tax
VCLT	Vienna Convention on the Law of Treaties
WTO	World Trade Organization

Contents

Chapter 1
The International Tax System at the Dawn of a Fundamental Reconsideration?

Abstract This introductory chapter outlines the contents of the forthcoming UN Framework Convention on International Tax Cooperation (FTC), as a challenge to OECD dominance in the governance of international taxation. It briefly sets out the FTC's objectives, principles, and commitments, emphasizing sustainable development, equity, and human rights as adopted via UN General Assembly resolutions in 2023 and 2024. The analysis explores the FTC's potential to reshape global tax governance, addressing North-South divides and the concerns of Low- and Middle-Income Countries (LMIC).

1.1 Introduction

On 22 December 2023 the General Assembly of the United Nations (UN) adopted UNGA resolution 78/230 to pursue an unprecedented development in international taxation; the creation of the United Nations Framework Convention on International Tax Cooperation (FTC).[1] Another major step followed on 16 August 2024 when the United Nations Ad Hoc Committee to Draft Terms of Reference for the United Nations Framework Convention on International Tax Cooperation (Ad Hoc Committee) voted to adopt its blueprint (Terms of Reference, TOR).[2] On 24 December 2024, the UNGA adopted the TOR.[3] While the final form of the FTC will be negotiated from 2025 through 2027, much of the contents of the prospective FTC is already fixed by these resolutions, particularly its key elements such as the objectives, the guiding principles and several of its main commitments. Even at this early

[1] United Nations General Assembly (UNGA) (2023b) (UNGA Res 78/230).

[2] United Nations General Assembly (UNGA) (2024a) (TOR) and United Nations General Assembly (UNGA) (2024c) (UNGA A/79/333).

[3] United Nations General Assembly (UNGA) (2024b) (UNGA Res 79/235), referring to UNGA A/79/333 (n 2 in this chapter) Annex I.

E. Vanderbruggen, *Reconstructing Global Tax Governance*, SpringerBriefs in Law, https://doi.org/10.1007/978-981-95-5617-5_1

stage the FTC has been heralded by its proponents as 'a historic victory'[4] 'bold'[5] 'a pivotal moment in history'[6] 'the cusp of significant change'[7] 'a key advancement'[8] 'unprecedented'.[9]

The FTC seeks to reshape the international tax system, once the bastion of sovereignty and voluntarism, with objectives, principles and commitments that have been given a new or enhanced role. For the first time, the FTC places certain community interests and principles in the central role for international tax cooperation, such as sustainable development, inclusive cooperation, human rights and international equity. The FTC can also be seen through the prism of the North-South divide as it started out as an initiative by LMICs against the Organisation for Economic Co-operation and Development (OECD)'s de-facto leadership in global tax affairs.

This monograph seeks to examine the principal elements of the FTC, as established by Resolution 79/235. The objectives, principles, and several key commitments, as well as the potential subjects for the FTC's protocols, as delineated in Resolution 79/235, provide a foundation for a preliminary analysis of the FTC's potential to reshape the landscape of international tax cooperation. A central focus of this work is the potential significance of the FTC's explicit linkage to core principles of the international community that exceed the bilateralist foundations of international tax rules—most notably the multifaceted objectives of sustainable development, fairness or equity, and respect for human rights—to the international tax system. The question arises whether these principles may influence the progressive development of international taxation, as foundational tenets guiding the formulation of new tax commitments, or perhaps as interpretative tools, through the principle of systemic integration, which may shape the interpretation of tax treaty[10] provisions. Following an examination of the opportunities and challenges for the FTC's proposed international tax system, concluding observations synthesize its ongoing development.

[4] Bou Mansour (2023).

[5] Dourado (2025), pp. 3, 4.

[6] Lammers (2025), p. 67.

[7] Titus (2025), pp. 85, 92.

[8] Parada (2024), p. 771.

[9] Christensen (2024), p. 2.

[10] In this monograph, 'tax treaty' refers to any international treaty that has tax as the main subject matter, including but not limited to double taxation agreements (DTA).

1.2 The United Nation's Push for the FTC

The genesis of the FTC is linked to the Group of 20 (G20) and OECD's Base Erosion and Profit Shifting Project (BEPS), a 'historic overhaul of the tax system'[11] which started in 2013 to address certain forms of international tax avoidance. As the OECD Project got underway with its 15-point action plan, a proposal to form a new global tax body, in effect challenging the OECD, was tabled at the UN International Conference on Financing for Development at Addis Ababa in 2015 among criticism that international tax cooperation should be 'more inclusive'. It was narrowly defeated.[12] Perhaps informed by the Addis Ababa developments, the G20/OECD broadened the multilateral platform for BEPS in 2016 by creating the Inclusive Framework (IF) for BEPS which is at the time of writing joined by 147 jurisdictions (not all of which are states). In 2021, the OECD pressed on its project with 'BEPS 2.0', or the Two Pillar Solution.

It is hard to overstate the importance of the BEPS Project to the world of international taxation. It aims not only to amend essentially all bilateral tax treaties instantaneously by the 'Multilateral Instrument', but also, in a later stage referred to as the 'Two Pillar Solution' to eliminate a good part of tax incentive policies around the world by what has been called the 'Global Minimum Tax' by mainstream media (Pillar Two), while creating a new way to tax and share tax revenue from the global digital economy (Pillar One). But gradually criticism and obstacles rose.[13] It is against this background of a major tax system overhaul mainly spearheaded by the OECD, but with a process and outcomes that are not welcomed by all LMICs, that a push for the FTC at the UN is triggered.

The first formal step was taken on 16 November 2022 by the African Group of States,[14] leading to General Assembly resolution 77/244 of 20 December 2022. At this stage, the Assembly only asks the Secretary-General to prepare a report on the 'Promotion of inclusive and effective international tax cooperation at the United Nations' (SG Report), but clearly in view of 'the possibility of developing an international framework or instrument' through the UN 'taking into full consideration existing international and multilateral arrangements'.[15] The Secretary-General returns a scathing analysis of the G20/OECD process and some of its outcomes, which the OECD found 'surprising and disappointing'.[16] The Secretary-General points out in the SG Report that most of the OECD Members are from Europe and the Americas and none are from Africa. It is also suggested that the OECD/G20 IF cannot be deemed fully inclusive, as it leaves out more than 60 UN of the 193 UN

[11] Baert (2024).

[12] Anyangwe (2015).

[13] Cooper (2021), p. 533.

[14] United Nations (2022a) (UN Doc A/C.2/77/L.11/Rev.1).

[15] United Nations (2023) (UNGA Res 77/244); United Nations (2022b) (UNGA UN GAOR 56th plenary meeting UN Doc A/77/PV.56 (2022) (resumed)), para 16 (UN Doc A/77/441).

[16] In a press report, the OECD calls the report 'surprising' and 'disappointing': Robin (2023).

Members. The SG Report furthermore argues that some OECD solutions have flaws in terms of effective implementation and agenda-setting.[17] More in general, the Secretary-General notes 'long-standing concerns that existing paradigms for international tax cooperation were not serving the needs of all countries', and that '[OECD Model Double Taxation Convention[18] rules] would tend to allocate taxing rights primarily to the developed country in treaties between developed and developing countries'.[19] The conclusion of the Secretary-General is that enhancing the UN's leadership in international tax cooperation is accordingly the best way forward for inclusive cooperation in tax matters, and a framework convention is one of the options for achieving that.

In following of the SG Report, a pivotal vote takes place at the Assembly on 22 December 2023, whereby the UN decided by means of resolution 78/230 to move ahead with the option of the framework convention and to create an Ad Hoc Committee to prepare its TOR. The resolution was passed with 111 in favour, 46 against and 10 abstentions. Most LMICs voted in favour of the resolution, and most OECD members voted against. The Ad Hoc Committee started work in March 2024 and, after two sessions, the TOR was completed and adopted by the Ad Hoc Committee with 110 to 8, with 44 abstentions and later, as was mentioned above, by the Assembly resolution 79/235. The votes against adopting the TOR were now reduced to only 8, namely Australia, Canada, Israel, Japan, New Zealand, Republic of Korea, United Kingdom of Great Britain and Northern Ireland, United States of America, while Argentina joined the 'against' votes for resolution 79/235. There was a remarkable change in the voting pattern between 78/230 in 2023 and 79/235 at the end of 2024. A considerable number of 'against' votes of mostly European Union (EU) Members moved instead to abstention.

1.3 The Contents of the Forthcoming Framework Tax Convention Is Largely Fixed by Resolution 79/235

On 16 August 2024, the Ad Hoc Committee voted to adopt the blueprint for the enhancement of the role of the United Nations in the global tax system.[20] The United Nations General Assembly Resolution A/RES/78/230 (Resolution 78/230) established an FTC to govern the international tax system, following decades of de-facto leadership by the OECD in world tax affairs.[21] To a large degree, the Assembly's

[17] Baker (2023), pp. 364, 365, who notes the Secretary-General made 'a devastating assessment' of the OECD's process.

[18] OECD (2017) (OECD Model).

[19] United Nations General Assembly (UNGA) (2023a) (SG Report), para 23.

[20] TOR (n 2 in this chapter).

[21] UNGA Res 78/230 (n 1 in this chapter).

adoption of the TOR by Resolution 79/235[22] locks in the objectives, principles and rules for the FTC.

Its preamble will refer not only to the key resolutions which have led up to the FTC but also to resolution 70/1 on sustainable development goals and 69/313 which embodies the Addis Ababa Action Agenda, already mentioned above. These resolutions should also be reflected in the text, the TOR states.

Next, the TOR sets out the objectives the drafters are to include in the FTC, apparently in an exhaustive manner. The objective (a) is 'to establish fully inclusive and effective international tax cooperation', which mainly just recalls the designation and trigger of the FTC project. Objective (b) is to '[e]stablish a system of governance for international tax cooperation capable of responding to existing and future tax and tax-related challenges on an ongoing basis', which is foreshadowed in the SG Report: 'a framework convention, would also be a legally binding multilateral instrument, but one that is "constitutive" in nature, in that it would establish an overall system of international tax governance'.[23] This objective can be understood from the fact that the governance choices at the OECD-led projects, including who gets to participate in decision making and setting agendas for cooperation, are at the root of the UN's push for the FTC.[24]

Objectives (a) and (b) shed light on how the system should work; inclusive, and with governance mechanics. It is left to objective (c) to state in the pursuit of which values the objectives should be seen, and these are striking:

> To establish an inclusive, fair, transparent, efficient, equitable, and effective international tax system for sustainable development, with a view to enhancing the legitimacy, certainty, resilience, and fairness of international tax rules, while addressing challenges to strengthening domestic resource mobilisation.[25]

Sustainable development constitutes the overall purpose of the international tax system that the FTC seeks to establish: '[t]o establish an […] international tax system *for* sustainable development' (emphasis added). The function and possible impact of sustainable development on the international tax system is explored below in this article. The other terms used in objective (c) invoke core principles reflecting various challenges in the international tax system that the UN is seeking to address with the FTC. 'Inclusive', 'legitimacy' and 'effective' clearly relate to the pursuit of broader and more meaningful participation particularly by LMICs. Domestic resource mobilisation (DRM) most often refers to problems that particularly LMICs face in improving their domestic tax system and revenues.[26]

The TOR continues with principles to be included in the FTC that will guide the achievement of the stated objectives. Principles constitute the direction to a

[22] UNGA Res 79/235 (n 3 in this chapter).

[23] SG Report (n 19 in this chapter), para 55.

[24] SG Report (n 19 in this chapter), paras 16, 39, 44.

[25] TOR (n 2 in this chapter), para 7(c); UNGA Res 70/1 (25 September 2015) UN Doc A/RES/70/1 (UNGA Res 70/1).

[26] United Nations (2015), para 22.

destination rather than spelling out the point of arrival.[27] Again, there is no indication that the drafters can or should include other or additional principles besides the nine principles listed:

(a) Be universal in approach and scope and should fully consider the different needs, priorities, and capacities of all countries, including LMICs, in particular countries in special situations;
(b) Recognize that every Member State has the sovereign right to decide its tax policies and practices, while also respecting the sovereignty of other Members in such matters;
(c) Be aligned, in the pursuit of international tax cooperation, with states' obligations under international human rights law;
(d) Take a holistic, sustainable development perspective that covers in a balanced and integrated manner economic, social and environmental policy aspects;
(e) Be sufficiently flexible, resilient and agile to ensure equitable and effective results as societies, technology and business models and the international tax cooperation landscapes evolve;
(f) Contribute to achieving sustainable development by ensuring fairness in allocation of taxing rights under the international tax system;
(g) Provide for rules that are as simple and easy to administer as the subject matter allows;
(h) Ensure certainty for taxpayers and governments;
(i) Require transparency and accountability of all taxpayers.

The TOR requires that the FTC will provide a number of commitments by its parties. Here, the drafters need to include at least the six commitments that are set out in the TOR, but this is not an exhaustive list. More commitments may be added:

(a) Fair allocation of taxing rights, including equitable taxation of multinational enterprises;
(b) Addressing tax evasion and avoidance by high-net worth individuals and ensuring their effective taxation in relevant Members;
(c) International tax cooperation approaches that will contribute to the achievement of sustainable development in its three dimensions, economic, social and environmental, in a balanced and integrated manner;
(d) Effective mutual administrative assistance in tax matters, including with respect to transparency and exchange of information for tax purposes;
(e) Addressing tax-related illicit financial flows, tax avoidance, tax evasion and harmful tax practices;
(f) Effective prevention and resolution of tax disputes.

Commitment (a) recalls one of the main the objectives of the FTC, the equitable division of global taxing rights. Several others reflect the challenges particularly

[27] Bodansky (1999), p. 19.

LMICs face addressing international tax avoidance and evasion, notably commitments (b), (d) and (e).

The TOR provides some additional instructions for the drafters of the FTC, on which this monograph will not elaborate, in relation to the secretariat that is to be formed, the conference of the parties, subsidiary bodies, financial resources, capacity building and other matters Finally, the negotiators need to prepare at least two legally independent instruments, i.e. protocols. The subject matter of the first two protocols has been selected from a limited list of four topics: 'taxation of cross-border services in an increasingly digitized economy' and 'the prevention and resolution of tax disputes'.[28]

References

Anyangwe, E. (2015). Glee, relief and regret: Addis Ababa outcome receives mixed reception. *The Guardian*. Retrieved January 31, 2025, from https://www.theguardian.com/global-development/2015/jul/16/outcome-document-addis-ababa-ffd3-financing-for-development

Baert, P. (2024). Balancing on two pillars: Global corporate tax reform. *European Parliamentary Research Service, Parliament of Europe*. https://www.europarl.europa.eu/portal/en

Baker, P. (2023). UN Secretary-General's Report on the promotion of inclusive and effective International Tax Cooperation at the United Nations. *British Tax Review, 4*(364), 365.

Bodansky, D. (1999). *The Framework Convention/Protocol Approach* (No. Paper 1; Technical Briefing Series). World Health Organization (WHO). https://iris.who.int/handle/10665/65355

Bou Mansour, M. (2023). UN adopts plans for historic tax reform. *Tax Justice Network*. Retrieved January 31, 2025, from https://taxjustice.net/press/un-adopts-plans-for-historic-tax-reform

Christensen, R. C. (2024). Between revolution and rhetoric: The UN vote and the future of International Tax Cooperation. *British Tax Review, 2*.

Cooper, G. S. (2021). Building on the rubble of pillar one. *Bulletin for International Taxation, 75*(11–12), 533.

Dourado, A. P. (2025). United Nations, International Tax Justice and mutual recognition of interests. *Intertax, 53*(1), 3, 4.

Lammers, J. (2025). Rebalancing power: A UN Tax Council as a political counterbalance. *Intertax, 53*(1), 67.

OECD. (2017). *UN Model Tax Convention on income and on capital: Condensed version 2017*. Organisation for Economic Cooperation and Development.

Parada, L. (2024). U.N. International Tax Cooperation: The terms of references final draft. *Tax Notes International, 116*(5), 771.

Robin, J. (2023). Report 'surprising' and 'disappointing': OECD surprised and disappointed over UN global tax-plan. *International Consortium of Investigative Journalists*. Retrieved January 31, 2025, from https://www.icij.org/investigations/paradise-papers/oecd-surprised-and-disappointed-over-un-global-tax-plan/

Titus, A. (2025). From Africa to the World: Pathways to inclusivity and political justice at the UN. *Intertax, 53*(1), 85, 92.

[28] The second of the two first protocols were decided in the Organizational Meeting in February 2025: United Nations (2025) (UN Doc A/AC.298/CRP.5). The potential other priority topics were measures against tax-related illicit financial flows and addressing tax evasion and avoidance by high-net worth individuals and ensuring their effective taxation in relevant Member States.

United Nations. (2015). *Resolution 69/313: Addis Ababa action agenda of the third international conference on financing for development* (No. UN Doc A/RES/69/313). United Nations. https://www.un.org/esa/ffd/wp-content/uploads/2015/08/AAAA_Outcome.pdf

United Nations. (2022a). *Promotion of inclusive and effective International Tax Cooperation at the United Nations: Nigeria revised draft resolution* (No. UN Doc A/C.2/77/L.11/Rev.1). United Nations General Assembly.

United Nations. (2022b). *Resolution: 77/441: Macroeconomic policy questions* (No. UN Doc A/77/441). United Nations General Assembly, Second Committee.

United Nations. (2023). *Resolution 77/244: Promotion of inclusive and effective International Tax Cooperation at the United Nations* (No. UN Doc A/RES/77/244). United Nations General Assembly.

United Nations. (2025). *Subject of Protocol II: Draft decision by the Chair* (No. UN Doc A/AC.298/CRP.5). Intergovernmental Negotiating Committee on the United Nations Framework Convention on International Tax Cooperation.

United Nations General Assembly (UNGA). (2023a). *Promotion of inclusive and effective International Tax Cooperation at the United Nations: Report of the Secretary-General 78/235 (SG Report)* (No. UN Doc A/78/235).

United Nations General Assembly (UNGA). (2023b). *Resolution 78/230: Promotion of inclusive and effective International Tax Cooperation at the United Nations* (No. UN Doc A/RES/78/230). United Nations General Assembly.

United Nations General Assembly (UNGA). (2024a). *Chair's proposal for draft terms of reference (TOR)* (No. UN Doc A/AC.295/2024/L.4.).

United Nations General Assembly (UNGA). (2024b). *Resolution 79/235* (No. UN Doc A/RES/79/235). United Nations General Assembly.

United Nations General Assembly (UNGA). (2024c). *Resolution 79/333: Promotion of inclusive and effective International Tax Cooperation at the United Nations* (No. UN Doc A/79/333). United Nations General Assembly.

Chapter 2
The Genesis and Evolution of the UN Framework Tax Convention: Challenging OECD-Led Tax Governance

Abstract This chapter traces the FTC's origins from the OECD's BEPS project in 2013, criticisms of its inclusivity, and key UN milestones like the 2015 Addis Agenda and UNGA resolutions from 2022 to 2024. It details the Ad Hoc Committee's work and highlights LMIC dissatisfaction and shifts toward UN-led governance.

The UN has made a significant contribution to international taxation since its creation in 1947, and in its previous incarnation as the League of Nations. For decades, the UN has shaped international taxation through the UN Model Tax Convention for the Avoidance of Double Taxation,[1] the Manual on Transfer Pricing,[2] and other important efforts led by the UN Committee of Experts on International Cooperation in Tax Matters (UN Tax Committee). Established as a subsidiary of the UN Department of Economic and Social Affairs,[3] the committee was renamed the Ad Hoc Committee in 2004 following the Monterrey Consensus, which urged enhanced dialogue among national tax authorities and greater coordination among multilateral bodies.[4] Under the Addis Agenda, the UN Tax Committee increased its meetings to two four-day sessions annually to strengthen international tax cooperation.[5]

[1] United Nations (2021).

[2] United Nations Department of Economic and Social Affairs (UNDESA) (2021).

[3] United Nations Department of Economic and Social Affairs (UNDESA) (n.d.).

[4] United Nations (2002).

[5] United Nations (2015), para 29.

E. Vanderbruggen, *Reconstructing Global Tax Governance*, SpringerBriefs in Law, https://doi.org/10.1007/978-981-95-5617-5_2

2.1 2013: The OECD Overhauls the International Tax System to Curb Base Erosion and Profit Shifting

Although LMICs have longstanding grievances with the distribution of global taxing rights, the UN's journey towards the FTC should be understood in connection with the BEPS. In 2013, at the behest of the G20, the OECD launched a major initiative to curb BEPS, with a 15-point Action Plan. This was later complemented by Pillar One (which focused on new tax rules for the digital economy) and Pillar Two (known for its 'Global Minimum Tax'). The BEPS project launched a 'historic overhaul of the tax system'[6] with a deluge of model laws, international instruments, draft conventions, and often complex technical guidance, all with the UN mostly on the sidelines.

2.2 2015: The Addis Agenda

A significant milestone unfolded at the UN International Conference on Financing for Development in Addis Ababa in 2015, where a bid to establish a global tax body was barely defeated.[7] Although the proposal did not succeed, the Addis Ababa Action Agenda[8] incorporates several tax-related issues, principles, and concerns that were later reflected in the TOR for the FTC. These encompass DRM through taxation,[9] the linkage between illicit financial flows (IFF) and tax avoidance,[10] and the allocation of taxing rights over multinational enterprises (MNEs).[11] Additionally, the Addis Agenda addresses the issue of 'excessive tax incentives, particularly in extractive industries',[12] while acknowledging that 'tax incentives can be an appropriate policy tool.'[13] It further commits to enhanced tax cooperation, including through information exchange and CbC reporting for MNEs.[14] In 2015, most UN Members did not explicitly advocate for a leading UN role in international tax cooperation.[15] However, several statements within the Addis Agenda signalled underlying dissatisfaction among some members with the OECD's stewardship of global tax initiatives:

---

[6] Baert (2024).

[7] Anyangwe (2015).

[8] United Nations (2015).

[9] Ibid, para 22.

[10] Ibid, para 23.

[11] Ibid.

[12] Ibid, para 26.

[13] Ibid, para 27.

[14] Ibid.

[15] Ibid, para 28.

> We stress that efforts in international tax cooperation should be universal in approach and scope and should fully take into account the different needs and capacities of all countries.[16]

2.3 2016: The Inclusive Framework Is Born

Following the narrowly defeated proposal to establish a global tax body at the 2015 UN International Conference on Financing for Development in Addis Ababa, the OECD and G20 extended invitations in 2016 to other states, including numerous LMICs, to participate in the BEPS initiative through the OECD/G20 IF.[17] By 2021, the IF, comprising 145 member and associate member jurisdictions, had developed the Pillar One and Pillar Two solutions. However, the IF faced criticism for insufficient opportunities for meaningful participation by LMICs.[18] Subsequently, intermittent calls for the creation of a UN tax body re-emerged, reflecting ongoing concerns about the inclusivity and efficacy of existing global tax frameworks.[19]

2.4 2020–2021: 'Slow Demolition' of the OECD/G20 BEPS Pillar One

BEPS Pillar One, which promised the reallocation of taxing rights worth more than 100 billion US$,[20] requires implementation through a multilateral treaty.[21] At the beginning of 2020, it became clear that the negotiations for this treaty were not proceeding as hoped. Professor Graeme Cooper notes 'a slow demolition' of the once ambitious proposed scope of Pillar One, including a drastic reduction in the number of enterprises to which the new rules on taxing digital income would apply and calculation of Amount A.[22] Although the OECD expected to reach a consensus by 2020 on Pillar One, that on crucial details remained elusive.[23]

---

[16] Ibid, para 28.

[17] OECD, 'All Interested Countries and Jurisdictions to be Invited to Join Global Efforts Led by the OECD and G20 to Close International Tax Loopholes' (Press release, 23 February 2016); Quiñones (2017), p. 165.

[18] Christians and Van Apeldoorn (2018), p. 226; United Nations General Assembly (UNGA) (2023a), paras 31–46.

[19] Whitehead (2016).

[20] OECD (2021).

[21] *Multilateral Convention to Implement Amount A of Pillar One*, not yet opened for signature (not yet in force).

[22] Cooper (2021).

[23] Ndubai (2019). On the challenges to finding consensus in general (in relation to pillar two), see Rosenzweig (2023), p. 83.

On 30 May 2024, the Co-Chairs of the OECD/G20 IF on BEPS reported that the IF was approaching the conclusion of negotiations on a comprehensive package for Pillar One, encompassing the text of the Multilateral Convention (MLC) for Amount A and a framework for Amount B.[24] In June 2024, the revised MLC text was submitted to the IF for adoption. Nevertheless, several unresolved issues persist with the Amount B framework, as highlighted in the Co-Chairs' update on 13 January 2025.[25] A primary concern is that the pricing matrix yields inappropriate outcomes for taxpayers engaged in baseline marketing and distribution activities, with no consensus solution yet endorsed by all members. Consequently, agreement on the Pillar One package within the IF remains elusive, as negotiations continue.

In contrast, Pillar Two of the OECD/G20 IF on BEPS, which establishes a global minimum Effective Tax Rate (ETR) of 15% for multinational groups with annual revenues exceeding €750 million, has shown progress, but also criticism.[26] The Global Anti-Base Erosion (GloBE) Rules, promulgated by the IF on 20 December 2021, have been successfully incorporated into domestic legislation with notable expediency. According to the central record updated on 31 March 2025, 32 countries or jurisdictions have attained transitional qualified status for their legislation under the GloBE Model Rules, encompassing the Income Inclusion Rule (IIR), the Undertaxed Payments Rule (UTPR), the Domestic Minimum Top-up Tax (DMTT), or the Qualified Domestic Minimum Top-up Tax (QDMTT) Safe Harbour.[27] Furthermore, negotiations on the Subject to Tax Rule (STTR), another critical component of Pillar Two, have culminated in a MLC, signed by nine countries as of 19 September 2024.[28]

In later developments, the United States withdraws on 20 January 2025, effected through an executive order declaring the agreement to have 'no force or effect' within the US. The decision was justified by concerns over the agreement's purported 'discriminatory' nature and its perceived assertion of 'extraterritorial jurisdiction' over the income of American companies.[29] The Trump administration directed the US Treasury to formulate a list of potential retaliatory measures. Subsequently, in February 2025, the US initiated investigations into digital services taxes (DSTs) imposed by foreign jurisdictions, aiming to safeguard American companies from extraterritorial fiscal authority.[30] With respect to Pillar Two, however, an understanding is reached on 28 June 2025 between the US and the G7 on a so-called "side by side" operation of Pillar Two with existing US Global Intangible Low-Taxed Income (GILTI) tax regime.[31]

---

[24] OECD (2024b).

[25] OECD (2025c).

[26] TNI (2021, 2023).

[27] OECD (2025a).

[28] OECD (2024a).

[29] Global Tax Deal (2025).

[30] OECD (2025b).

[31] Department of Finance Canada (2025).

2.5 2022: Proposal by the African Group and Resolution 77/244

On 16 November 2022, Nigeria, representing the African Group of States, introduced a draft resolution at the United Nations.[32] On 20 December 2022, the General Assembly adopted Resolution 77/244, which contemplated 'the possibility of developing an international framework or instrument' under the UN's auspices, while 'taking into full consideration existing international and multilateral arrangements'.[33] The resolution mandated the SG Report by the Secretary-General.

2.6 2023: A 'Surprising and Disappointing'[34] Report by the Secretary-General, Culminating in Resolution 78/230

The SG Report, issued on 26 July 2023, elucidates the concepts of 'inclusive' and 'effective' in the context of international tax cooperation.[35] The SG Report evaluates the efforts of the United Nations and the OECD, particularly through the OECD/G20 IF on BEPS and the Global Forum on Transparency and Exchange of Information for Tax Purposes (Global Forum). It concludes, based on its analysis and stakeholder input, that the participation of LMICs in OECD-led initiatives remains insufficiently inclusive and exhibits deficiencies in effective implementation.[36] The SG Report advocates for enhanced UN engagement as the optimal pathway to advance international tax cooperation, proposing three potential approaches: a convention, a framework convention, and a cooperation framework. While the Secretary-General refrains from explicitly endorsing any single option, the SG Report notes that 'a coordination function [...] provides less of the certainty necessary to create a sufficiently stable international tax system'.[37] Furthermore, it highlights the successful application of the framework convention approach in other domains,[38] such as climate change.[39]

Following the issuance of the SG Report, deliberations on the three proposed options for advancing international tax cooperation commenced within the United Nations. The United Kingdom advocated for a framework cooperation model over

---

[32] United Nations (2022a).

[33] United Nations (2022b), para 16.

[34] In a press report, the OECD calls the report 'surprising' and 'disappointing: Robin (2023).

[35] United Nations General Assembly (UNGA) (2023a).

[36] Baker (2023), who notes the Secretary-General made 'a devastating assessment' of the OECD's process.

[37] United Nations General Assembly (UNGA) (2023a), para 52.

[38] United Nations General Assembly (UNGA) (2023a), para 57.

[39] United Nations Framework Convention on Climate Change (adopted 9 May 1992, entered into force 21 March 1994) 1771 UNTS 107 (UNFCCC).

a framework convention, but this proposal was rejected.[40] Switzerland expressed reservations, stating that a binding framework convention would 'not achieve the desired outcome'.[41] In contrast, statements from several LMICs underscored the depth of their dissatisfaction and their resolve to address systemic issues, as articulated in the following:

> It is high time that the international community rectifies the injustice in global taxing rights, which impoverishes millions and traces its origins to the League of Nations era, when most Member States were colonies. This inequity has been perpetuated by the dominance of affluent nations' coalitions in international rulemaking.[42]

On 22 December 2023, the UN General Assembly adopted Resolution 78/230, endorsing the framework convention approach and establishing an Ad Hoc Committee to draft its TOR. The resolution passed with 111 votes in favour, 46 against, and 10 abstentions.[43] The majority of LMICs supported the resolution, while most OECD Members voted in opposition.

2.7 2024: Terms of Reference by the Ad Hoc Committee

The Ad Hoc Committee commenced its work in 2024.[44] The First Session of the Ad Hoc Committee to Draft TOR for an FTC was convened from 26 April to 8 May 2024, encompassing 16 meetings at UN Headquarters in New York. Following this session, the Chair and Bureau formulated a 'Zero Draft' of the TOR.[45] The Second Session, held from 29 July to 16 August 2024 at UN Headquarters in New York, comprised 31 online meetings during which participating states provided input on the Zero Draft TOR. On 15 August 2024, the Chair presented a proposed TOR, which the Committee adopted through a vote on 16 August 2024.[46] The vote resulted in 110 states in favour, 44 abstentions, and eight states opposing (Australia, Canada, Israel, Japan, New Zealand, Republic of Korea, United Kingdom, and United States).[47] Notably, compared to the previous year's vote on Resolution 78/230,

---

[40] United Nations General Assembly (UNGA) (2023b).

[41] United Nations General Assembly (UNGA) (2023c).

[42] Ibid South Africa.

[43] United Nations General Assembly (UNGA) (2023d), p. 7.

[44] This book frequently refers to the verbal statements made by participating states at the Ad Hoc Committee as documented in the video and audio recordings, which are available on the UN website. The video recordings for the First and Second Sessions are available at the following links, respectively: United Nations (2024a, 2024b, 2024c). All written Inputs to the Second Session are available here <https://financing.desa.un.org/un-tax-convention/second-session>.

[45] United Nations Department of Economic and Social Affairs (UNDESA) (2024) (Zero Draft TOR).

[46] United Nations General Assembly (UNGA) (2024a).

[47] United Nations General Assembly (UNGA) (2024b).

several states, including members of the EU,[48] shifted their stance from opposition to abstention.

2.8 2025: Protocols and Organizational Meetings

The Intergovernmental Negotiating Committee (INC) for the FTC convened its organisational session from 3 to 6 February 2025, initiating a 3-year process comprising at least three substantive sessions annually, each spanning up to 10 working days, to negotiate the FTC and two protocols addressing priority issues. During the 4-day organisational session, the Chair and Bureau were elected, and several critical matters were resolved.

However, the United States delegation withdrew from the negotiations on the first day, asserting that 'the objectives of a future FTC are incompatible with U.S. priorities' and expressing a rejection of 'the very nature of these discussions' as well as any outcomes arising from the process.[49]

A key objective of the organisational session was to determine the subject of the second early protocol to the FTC. While the TOR previously agreed upon by UN Members designated the first protocol to address the taxation of income from cross-border services in an increasingly digitalised and globalised economy,[50] the topic for the second protocol required selection from a list of priority areas outlined in the TOR. These included taxation of the digitalised economy, measures to combat tax-related IFF, prevention and resolution of tax disputes, and addressing tax evasion and avoidance by high-net-worth individuals to ensure their effective taxation in relevant Members.[51] The selection of the second protocol's topic proved relatively straightforward, with the prevention and resolution of tax disputes chosen, in part due to its perception as the 'least controversial' option.[52]

A contentious issue during the organisational session of the FTC was the determination of the voting procedure. The African Group, alongside numerous other Members, advocated strongly for decision-making by simple majority vote. Conversely, the EU and other parties underscored the primacy of consensus-based decision-making. This matter dominated the session's agenda, culminating in a resolution that decisions would primarily be made by consensus. However, in instances where consensus proves unattainable, a two-thirds majority would be required to adopt decisions on substantive matters. While some viewed this outcome as a triumph for inclusivity, particularly for LMICs, others contended that

[48] The EU and its prospective members moved to 'abstention', as did Turkey. Australia, Canada, Israel, Japan, New Zealand, Republic of Korea and the UK, and the US remained 'against'.

[49] United Nations (2025).

[50] United Nations General Assembly (UNGA) (2024a), para 15.

[51] Ibid, para 16.

[52] International Institute for Sustainable Development (IISD) (n.d.-c).

decision-making by vote could undermine the widespread adoption and implementation of future agreements.[53]

The organisational session also established rules for multi-stakeholder participation, facilitating the involvement of 'relevant non-governmental organisations, civil society organisations, academic institutions, the private sector, and other stakeholders' on a non-objection basis.[54]

Following the session, on 4 April 2025, the INC issued a roadmap and working methods for the development of the FTC and its two protocols,[55] alongside guidelines for organising intersessional work.[56] The roadmap delineates a schedule for the development process, with milestones for each workstream spanning March 2025 to July 2027. The guidelines underscore the necessity of clearly defined work plans to avoid duplication and ensure comprehensive stakeholder input.

The inaugural substantive session of the INC was convened from 4 to 8 August 2025 in New York, following an initial public briefing and a series of stakeholder consultations. This landmark session saw active engagement from over 100 Members and was structured around three workstreams corresponding to the FTC and its two protocols. Discussions centred on critical issues, including the equitable allocation of taxing rights, fair taxation of multinational enterprises, effective mechanisms for preventing and resolving tax disputes, and approaches to international tax cooperation that advance sustainable development. The African Group consistently emphasized the need for a genuinely inclusive process to rectify historical imbalances in global tax architectures, advocating for taxation aligned with the location of economic activity and value creation, alongside robust dispute resolution mechanisms and effective taxation of natural resources. The session also highlighted challenges faced by LMICs, such as limited tax treaty networks, high compliance costs, and insufficient consideration of capacity constraints in peer reviews, particularly in the context of mutual administrative assistance and information exchange. Overall, the session underscored the imperative to reform the existing international tax system and establish a framework that prioritises DRM for sustainable development.[57]

The second substantive session, taking place from 11 to 15 August 2025 in New York, focused on drafting the UN FTC and its two early protocols (the three workstreams).[58]

Regarding the first protocol on cross-border services, delegates discussed the taxing right of a country with regards to a company without a physical office, factory, or other permanent presence in that country, in terms of what kind of

---

[53] Ibid.

[54] Ibid.

[55] Intergovernmental Negotiating Committee on the United Nations Framework Convention on International Tax Cooperation (2025b).

[56] Intergovernmental Negotiating Committee on the United Nations Framework Convention on International Tax Cooperation (2025a).

[57] Tax Justice Network Africa (2025).

[58] International Institute for Sustainable Development (IISD) (n.d.-b).

connection-or nexus-should determine this right and how broad it should be. It is also debated whether to tax gross revenue or net profits, whether different sectors should be treated differently due to their inherent characteristics. The definition of 'services' was discussed as well, in the concern that it should be able to cover both existing business models and future emerging ones.[59]

In the discussion on the second protocol on dispute prevention and resolution, it was widely agreed that prevention should be prioritized. The need to close information gaps was highlighted, in order to ensure that tax administrations have early access to data. Delegates also considered whether the protocol should be mandatory for signatory countries, whether it should be an overarching framework for the Convention or embedded within each protocol, and how flexible should countries be in choosing dispute resolution mechanisms.[60]

Concluding the session, the Chair announced that the third substantive session will take place in Nairobi in November 2025. Meanwhile, the three workstreams will continue to develop preliminary proposals to be presented in that session.[61]

2.9 The Plans for 2026 and 2027

The member state-led negotiating committee is expected to spend most of 2026 and 2027 negotiating and drafting the FTC and the two first protocols, hopefully culminating in final texts by the 2027–2028 session. The General Assembly will then be able to adopt the FTC, after which it is opened for signature and ratification by all Members.

References

Anyangwe, E. (2015). Glee, relief and regret: Addis Ababa outcome receives mixed reception. *The Guardian*. Retrieved January 31, 2025, from https://www.theguardian.com/global-development/2015/jul/16/outcome-document-addis-ababa-ffd3-financing-for-development

Baert, P. (2024). Balancing on two pillars: Global corporate tax reform. *European Parliamentary Research Service, Parliament of Europe*. https://www.europarl.europa.eu/portal/en

Baker, P. (2023). UN Secretary-General's Report on the promotion of inclusive and effective international tax cooperation at the United Nations. *British Tax Review, 4*(364), 365.

Christians, A., & Van Apeldoorn, L. (2018). The OECD Inclusive Framework. *Bulletin for International Taxation, 72*, 226. https://doi.org/10.59403/288pdc

Cooper, G. S. (2021). Building on the Rubble of Pillar One. *Bulletin for International Taxation, 75*(11–12), 533.

[59] International Institute for Sustainable Development (IISD) (n.d.-a).

[60] Ibid.

[61] IBFD (2025).

Department of Finance Canada. (2025). G7 statement on global minimum taxes available. *Government of Canada*. Retrieved September 1, 2025, from https://www.canada.ca/en/department-finance/news/2025/06/g7-statement-on-global-minimum-taxes.html

Global Tax Deal. (2025). The Organization for Economic Co-operation and Development (OECD) global tax deal. *The White House*. Retrieved August 10, 2025, from https://www.whitehouse.gov/presidential-actions/2025/01/the-organization-for-economic-co-operation-and-development-oecd-global-tax-deal-global-tax-deal/

IBFD. (2025). *UN Tax Convention Wraps Second Session*. Retrieved September 8, 2025, from https://www.ibfd.org/news/un-tax-convention-wraps-second-session

Intergovernmental Negotiating Committee on the United Nations Framework Convention on International Tax Cooperation. (2025a). *Guidelines for intersessional work* (No. UN Doc A/AC.298/CRP.13).

Intergovernmental Negotiating Committee on the United Nations Framework Convention on International Tax Cooperation. (2025b). *Roadmap and working methods* (No. UN Doc A/AC.298/CRP.12).

International Institute for Sustainable Development (IISD). (n.d.-a). *Inside the UN Tax Convention Negotiations*. Retrieved September 8, 2025, from https://www.iisd.org/inside-un-tax-convention-negotiations

International Institute for Sustainable Development (IISD). (n.d.-b). *Second substantive session of INC for UN Framework Convention on International Tax Cooperation*. Retrieved October 8, 2025, from https://sdg.iisd.org/events/second-substantive-session-of-inc-for-un-framework-convention-on-international-tax-cooperation/?utm_source=chatgpt.com

International Institute for Sustainable Development (IISD). (n.d.-c). *Summary report, 3–6 February 2025: Organizational Session for the Intergovernmental Negotiations for the UN Framework Convention on International Tax Cooperation*. Retrieved October 8, 2025, from https://enb.iisd.org/un-framework-convention-international-tax-cooperation-organizational-session-summary

Ndubai, J. (2019, November 28). If developing countries are not listened to at the OECD, they will vote with their feet. *International Centre for Tax & Development*. Retrieved July 22, 2025, from https://www.ictd.ac/blog/developing-countries-oecd-inclusive-framework-consensus/

OECD. (2021). *130 Countries and jurisdictions join bold new framework for international tax reform*.

OECD. (2024a). *Signatories and parties to the Multilateral Convention to facilitate the implementation of the pillar two subject to tax rule*. Retrieved August 10, 2025, from https://www.oecd.org/content/dam/oecd/en/topics/policy-sub-issues/sttr/sttr-mli-signatories-and-parties.pdf

OECD. (2024b). *Statement by the co-chairs of the OECD/G20 inclusive framework on BEPS*. Newsroom. Retrieved August 10, 2025, from https://www.oecd.org/en/about/news/announcements/2024/05/statement-by-the-co-chairs-of-the-oecdg20-inclusive-framework-on-beps.html

OECD. (2025a). *Central record of legislation with transitional qualified status*. Global Minimum Tax. Retrieved August 10, 2025, from https://www.oecd.org/en/topics/sub-issues/global-minimum-tax/central-record-of-legislation-with-transitional-qualified-status.html

OECD. (2025b). Defending American companies and innovators from overseas extortion and unfair fines and penalties. *The White House*. Retrieved August 10, 2025, from https://www.whitehouse.gov/presidential-actions/2025/02/defending-american-companies-and-innovators-from-overseas-extortion-and-unfair-fines-and-penalties/

OECD. (2025c). *Pillar one update from the co-chairs of the inclusive framework on BEPS*. Newsroom. Retrieved August 10, 2025, from https://www.oecd.org/en/about/news/announcements/2025/01/pillar-one-update-co-chair-statement-oecd-g20-inclusive-framework-on-beps.html

Quiñones, N. (2017). The birth of a new International Tax Framework and the role of developing countries.

Robin, J. (2023). *Report 'surprising' and 'disappointing: OECD surprised and disappointed over UN Global Tax-Plan.* International Consortium of Investigative Journalists. Retrieved January 31, 2025, from https://www.icij.org/investigations/paradise-papers/oecd-surprised-and-disappointed-over-un-global-tax-plan/

Rosenzweig, A. H. (2023). BEPS: Endgame. *University of Memphis Law Review, 54*, 83.

Tax Justice Network Africa. (2025). *Updates from the First Session of the historic Intergovernmental Negotiating Committee (INC) on the United Nations Framework Convention on International Tax Cooperation.* Retrieved August 10, 2025, from https://taxjusticeafrica.net/resources/news/updates-first-session-historic-intergovernmental-negotiating-committee-inc-united-0

TNI. (2021). *OECD Global Tax Agreement Draws Mixed Reactions.*

TNI. (2023). *ASEAN Investment Ministers call for Global Minimum Tax Review.*

United Nations. (2002). *Report of the International Conference on Financing for Development* (No. Sales No. E.02.II.A.7; p. chap. I, resolution 1, annex).

United Nations. (2015). *Resolution 69/313: Addis Ababa action agenda of the third international conference on financing for development* (No. UN Doc A/RES/69/313). United Nations. https://www.un.org/esa/ffd/wp-content/uploads/2015/08/AAAA_Outcome.pdf

United Nations. (2021). *United Nations Model Double Taxation Convention between HICs and LMICs* (No. UN Doc. ST/ESA/340). United Nations.

United Nations. (2022a). *Promotion of inclusive and effective International Tax Cooperation at the United Nations: Nigeria revised draft resolution* (No. UN Doc A/C.2/77/L.11/Rev.1). United Nations General Assembly.

United Nations. (2022b). *Resolution: 77/441: Macroeconomic policy questions* (No. UN Doc A/77/441). United Nations General Assembly, Second Committee.

Inputs to the First Session: United Nations Ad Hoc Committee to Draft Terms of Reference for a United Nations Framework Convention on International Tax Cooperation. https://financing.desa.un.org/un-tax-convention/first-session

Inputs to the Second Session: United Nations Committee to Draft Terms of Reference for a United Nations Framework Convention on International Tax Cooperation. https://financing.desa.un.org/un-tax-convention/second-session

United Nations. (2025). *Statement at the Session for the Intergovernmental Negotiating Committee on the UN Framework Convention on International Tax Cooperation.* United States Mission to the United Nations. Retrieved August 10, 2025, from https://usun.usmission.gov/statement-at-the-session-for-the-intergovernmental-negotiating-committee-on-the-un-framework-convention-on-international-tax-cooperation/

United Nations Department of Economic and Social Affairs (UNDESA). (2021). *UN Practical Manual on Transfer Pricing for LMICs* (No. (ST/ESA/347)).

United Nations Department of Economic and Social Affairs (UNDESA). (2024, June 7). *Bureau's proposal for the zero draft terms of reference for a United Nations Framework Convention on International Tax Cooperation.* Financing for Sustainable Development Office.

United Nations Department of Economic and Social Affairs (UNDESA). (n.d.). *ECOSOC Resolution 2004/69 on Committee of Experts on International Cooperation in Tax Matters.* Retrieved September 8, 2025, from https://www.un.org/en/ecosoc/docs/2004/resolution%202004-69.pdf

United Nations General Assembly (UNGA). (2023a). *Promotion of inclusive and effective international tax cooperation at the United Nations: Report of the Secretary-General 78/235 (SG Report)* (No. UN Doc A/78/235).

United Nations General Assembly (UNGA). (2023b). *Promotion of inclusive and effective International Tax Cooperation at the United Nations: United Kingdom of Great Britain and Northern Ireland: Amendment to Draft Resolution* (No. UN Doc A/C.2/78/L. CRP.7). United Nations.

United Nations General Assembly (UNGA). (2023c). *Second Committee approves nine draft resolutions, including texts on International Tax Cooperation, External Debt, Global Climate, Poverty Eradication* (No. GA/EF/3597). Retrieved March 11, 2025, from https://press.un.org/en/2023/gaef3597.doc.htm

United Nations General Assembly (UNGA). (2023d). *UNGA official records* (No. UN Doc A/78/PV.50; p. 7). Resumption 1.

United Nations General Assembly (UNGA). (2024a). *Chair's proposal for draft terms of reference (TOR)* (No. UN Doc A/AC.295/2024/L.4.).

United Nations General Assembly (UNGA). (2024b). *Resolution 79/333: Promotion of inclusive and effective International Tax Cooperation at the United Nations* (No. UN Doc A/79/333). United Nations General Assembly.

Whitehead, F. (2016). Ecuador's foreign minister steps up campaign for UN Tax Body. *The Guardian*. Retrieved July 22, 2025, from https://www.theguardian.com/global-development/2016/sep/21/ecuador-foreign-minister-guillaume-long-steps-up-campaign-for-un-tax-body

Chapter 3
The Motivations Behind the Framework Tax Convention

Abstract Driven by LMIC grievances, the FTC addresses inequities in taxing rights favoring HICs, challenges in taxing digital services without physical presence, and exclusion from OECD processes. The chapter critiques legacy rules like the 1920s compromise, OECD's dominance, and BEPS outcomes, underscoring the role of the lack of inclusivity in global tax governance in the genesis of the FTC.

As is apparent from the SG Report,[1] which played an important role in the genesis of the FTC,[2] its conception has been driven by a combination of three overlapping factors: (1) a long-held view that the legacy distribution of taxing rights is not equitable,[3] (2) the rise of the digital economy and services industry, and (3) discontent with the process (particularly the lack of inclusion) and outcomes of the OECD's BEPS Project.

3.1 The 'Inequity' of the International Tax System

The SG Report noted 'a broader discontent rooted in the long-standing conviction by many countries and stakeholders that the existing tax treaty rules do not reserve sufficient taxing rights to countries hosting multinational enterprises and constituting markets for their products'.[4]

The foundational rules determining which country may tax specific revenue streams are primarily enshrined in Double Taxation Agreements (DTAs), which are

[1] United Nations General Assembly (UNGA) (2023a), para 23.

[2] Baker (2023), who notes the Secretary-General made 'a devastating assessment' of the OECD's process. The Report was requested as part of Nigeria and the African Group's draft resolution UN Doc A/C.2/77/L.11/Rev.1 (United Nations, 2022), later adopted as UNGA Res 77/244 (United Nations, 2023b).

[3] See also Roelofsen (2024), pp. 9–18.

[4] United Nations General Assembly (UNGA) (2023a), para 5.

E. Vanderbruggen, *Reconstructing Global Tax Governance*, SpringerBriefs in Law, https://doi.org/10.1007/978-981-95-5617-5_3

largely modelled on OECD frameworks with certain variations introduced by the United Nations, and in the OECD Transfer Pricing Guidelines (TPG). Extensive scholarly literature examines whether these rules disproportionately disadvantage LMICs.[5] Several scholars contend that the '1920s compromise'—balancing residence and source-based taxation—is outdated, inherently flawed, and inconsistent.[6]

As Professor Klaus Vogel argued in 1988, 'the contention that the present system of international income taxation is unjust and detrimental to the state applying this system is not unfounded'.[7]

In practice, these fundamental rules dictate the allocation of taxing rights among states, but economic disparities often result in unequal outcomes, favouring certain countries over others. Although these rules are designed to be objective and reciprocal, economic differences undermine their equitable application. Similarly, the TPG's rationale posits that valuable inputs—such as financing, intellectual property, software, management, technology, and highly skilled labour—warrant specific income or profit allocations. However, the economic reality is that such inputs are predominantly concentrated in high-income countries (HICs), exacerbating inequities in tax revenue distribution.[8]

3.2 Taxing Services and the Digital Economy

The preferential position of HICs in taxing services and digital businesses constitutes a significant impetus for the FTC.[9] LMICs perceive that HICs enjoy an advantage in the taxation of online and remote services. The OECD Model Tax Convention does not permit source-based taxation for services lacking a physical nexus to the country from which the income is derived. As articulated by India:

> In the digital economy, developing countries are frequently disadvantaged, facing challenges in taxing services provided by foreign entities without a physical presence within their jurisdictions.[10]

In response, in 2020, the UN Tax Committee introduced Article 12B to the UN Model DTA, enabling source taxation of 'automated digital services'. However, implementing this provision through bilateral treaty renegotiations could take decades, unless an expedited mechanism, with somewhat similar aims as the

[5] Christians and van Apeldoorn (2021), pp. 37–61; Avi-Yonah (2014), p. 1; Genschel (2002), p. 245; Ganghof (2006); Rosenzweig (2015), p. 373; Ozai (2025), pp. 639, 642.

[6] Graetz (2001), pp. 1357, 1363; Avi-Yonah et al. (2022), p. 279; Jimenez (2018), p. 620; Haque (2023), p. 80; Devereux and Vella (2014), p. 449.

[7] Vogel (1988), p. 216.

[8] For nuance on these assertions, see on this subject below Sect. 7.3.1.

[9] The OECD Model (2017b) has no tax at source for services without any physical connection. In 2020, the UN Committee of Experts on International Tax Matters decided to include a new article 12B in the 2001 UN Model DTA, allowing a source tax on 'automated digital services'.

[10] India, 3rd meeting of the First Session (29 April 2024) (n 44 in Chap. 2).

OECD's Multilateral Instrument (MLI)[11] for amending DTAs, is adopted. The first early protocol of the FTC, to be developed concurrently with the FTC itself, could potentially serve as such a mechanism to accelerate implementation.

During the Ad Hoc Committee's deliberations, Brazil proposed the inclusion of provisions for revenue-sharing agreements among states to ensure equitable distribution of digital taxes collected in one jurisdiction across countries *where economic activity occurs*.[12] Within the framework of the OECD/G20 BEPS Project, Pillar One sought to reallocate taxing rights over the digital economy. However, as highlighted in the SG Report, dissatisfaction with the progress and outcomes of Pillar One extends beyond LMICs to a broader array of states.[13] Faccio and Ghosh succinctly encapsulate this sentiment:

> We are essentially ceding revenue to large corporations due to an outdated tax architecture that no longer serves its intended purpose.[14]

Notably, the Ad Hoc Committee selected the taxation of cross-border services—a topic frequently addressed by the UN Tax Committee—as the focus for the first early protocol[15] of the FTC.[16] The African Group advocated that a protocol addressing the digital economy would represent 'a quick win for all involved'.[17] The Committee deliberately avoided a detailed definition of 'services'[18] or clarification of potential overlaps with the 'taxation of the digitalised economy'. One potential approach is a protocol establishing source taxation for all cross-border services, which could garner support from a significant and increasing number of states. Such a protocol might serve as a mechanism to facilitate the mass amendment of bilateral tax treaties.[19]

---

[11] OECD (2017a) (signed 7 June 2017, entered into force 1 July 2018) OECD/LEGAL/0432 (MLI).

[12] Brazil, 11th meeting of the First Session (3 May 2024) (n 44 in Chap. 2); Gonzalez-Barreda (2018), p. 278.

[13] United Nations General Assembly (UNGA) (2023a), para 36; Avi-Yonah et al. (2022).

[14] Faccio and Ghosh (2024), p. 358.

[15] United Nations General Assembly (UNGA) (2024). 110 states voted in favour with 44 abstentions and 8 votes against (Australia, Canada, Israel, Japan, New Zealand, the Republic of Korea, the United Kingdom and the United States. The voting pattern notably changed compared to Resolution 78/230, the key vote to move ahead with the FTC in 2023 as the EU members (and prospective members, plus Turkyie) moved from 'against' in 2023 to 'abstention' in 2024: UNGA Res 78/230 [United Nations General Assembly (UNGA), 2023b], arts 15–17: 'taxation of income derived from the provision of cross-border services in an increasingly digitalized and globalized economy'; the remaining subject matters are the digital economy, IFF, and taxation of high-net-worth individuals, environmental challenges, exchange of information, mutual assistance and harmful tax practices.

[16] United Nations (2023a) (Co-Coordinators' Report).

[17] African Group, Inputs to the Second Session (n 44 in Chap. 2), para 15.

[18] South Africa, 12th Meeting of the First Session (3 May 2024) (n 44 in Chap. 2).

[19] According to the International Bureau of Fiscal Documentation, a significant number of DTAs contains source taxation on fees for technical services, notably 40% of non-OECD/non-OECD DTAs, 22% of non-OECD/OECD DTAs and 8% of OECD/OECD DTAs. This data was based on the period between 2010 and 2023: IBFD inputs (n 44 in Chap. 2).

3.3 Lack of Inclusion in International Tax Decision Making

The dissatisfaction of LMICs centres on the dominance of OECD leadership in global taxation.[20] In his opening remarks, the Chair of the Ad Hoc Committee cautioned against 'allowing a few states or organisations to dictate their rules'.[21] Jamaica echoed this sentiment, stating: 'It is evident that the international tax system, as developed over decades, was designed and negotiated primarily by HICs, often proving incompatible with the DRM challenges faced by developing countries within an inherently unequal tax framework'.[22] Brazil concurred, asserting: 'For too long, the voices of developing countries have been marginalised in international tax discussions.'[23]

The SG Report observed that all 38 member countries of the OECD are classified as upper-middle- or high-income economies. At the time, the OECD/IF encompassed 143 member jurisdictions, including 17 overseas territories,[24] thereby excluding 67 sovereign states. The SG Report critiques the OECD's initiatives for insufficiently addressing the priorities and needs of LMICs.[25] For instance, the Global Forum, with 168 member jurisdictions, encounters significant implementation challenges in LMICs, particularly with respect to the Common Reporting Standard, which many find difficult to adopt effectively.[26]

Scholars, including Rasmus Corlin Christensen, Martin Hearson, and Tovony Randriamanalina, have further highlighted the limited capacity of LMICs to engage meaningfully in OECD processes.[27] Their interviews with IF representatives from LMICs revealed multiple barriers to full participation, including insufficient financial resources to attend meetings, time constraints, and a lack of technical expertise. In essence, as they note, 'developing countries are at the table, but very little is on the menu'.[28]

While dissatisfaction with the OECD served as a catalyst, many LMICs were resolute in asserting greater influence in international tax policy, irrespective of inclusivity challenges. A significant, albeit unsuccessful, effort to establish a UN tax

---

[20] United Nations General Assembly (UNGA) (2023a), para 5.

[21] Chair opening remarks, 1st Meeting of the First Session (26 April 2024) (n 44 in Chap. 2).

[22] Jamaica, 1st Meeting of the First Session (26 April 2024) (n 44 in Chap. 2).

[23] Brazil, 4th meeting of the First Session (29 April 2024) (n 44 in Chap. 2).

[24] As far as The Netherlands is concerned, for example, there are three member jurisdictions: The Netherlands, Aruba and Curacao. See the analysis by Oei (2022), p. 199.

[25] United Nations General Assembly (UNGA) (2023a), paras 33–4, 40. It has regularly been raised that not all issues prioritized by the OECD or IF are also priorities of developing states: Peters (2015); Herzfeld (2017), pp. 29–36; Rocha (2017), pp. 179, 190–196, para 9.04.

[26] United Nations General Assembly (UNGA) (2023a), paras 39–44.

[27] Ozai (2020), pp. 53–54; Brauner (2022), p. 1; Harpaz (2023), p. 1007; Fung (2017), p. 76; Christians and Van Apeldoorn (2018); United Nations General Assembly (UNGA) (2023a), paras 31–46; Christensen et al. (2020).

[28] Christensen et al. (2020).

body occurred at the 2015 Addis Ababa Summit, predating the inauguration of the OECD/G20 IF in Kyoto in June 2016.

Despite the critiques outlined in the SG Report, HICs failed to achieve consensus by the deadline for the Multilateral Convention on Amount A. Notably, LMICs succeeded in engaging meaningfully within this forum, notwithstanding reported obstacles. Other issues highlighted in the SG Report primarily concern practical and implementation challenges, including delays, complexity, and logistical barriers for LMICs.[29] Such practical difficulties are inevitable when pursuing international tax reforms.

A fundamental critique in the SG Report pertains to the 'pre-conditions' imposed on LMICs for participation in international tax forums, such as adherence to the minimum standards of the OECD/G20 IF and the commitment to implement Exchange of Information on Request within the Global Forum.[30] While this may hold in theory, the SG Report does not assess whether these minimum standards were already deemed acceptable by LMICs.

References

Avi-Yonah, R. S. (2014). Corporate taxation and corporate social responsibility. *New York University Journal of Law & Business, 11*(1), 1.

Avi-Yonah, R. S., Kim, Y. R. (Christine), & Sam, K. (2022). A new framework for digital taxation. *Harvard International Law Journal, 63*(2), 279.

Baker, P. (2023). UN Secretary-General's Report on the promotion of inclusive and effective international tax cooperation at the United Nations. *British Tax Review, 4*(364), 365.

Brauner, Y. (2022). Serinity now! The (not so) inclusive framework and the multilateral instrument. *Florida Tax Review, 26*, 1.

Christensen, R. C., Hearson, M., & Randriamanalina, T. (2020). *At the table, off the menu: Assessing the participation of lower-income countries in global tax negotiations* (No. Working Paper 115). International Centre of Tax and Development, Institute of Development Studies. https://www.ictd.ac/publication/table-off-menu-participation-lower-income-countries-tax-negotiations

Christians, A., & Van Apeldoorn, L. (2018). The OECD Inclusive Framework. *Bulletin for International Taxation, 72*, 226. https://doi.org/10.59403/288pdc

Christians, A., & Van Apeldoorn, L. (2021). *Tax cooperation in an unjust world*. In *Tax cooperation in an unjust world* (pp. 37–61). Oxford University Press.

Devereux, M., & Vella, J. (2014). Are we heading towards a corporate tax system fit for the 21st century? *Fiscal Studies & Intertax, 35*(4), 449.

Faccio, T., & Ghosh, J. (2024). Why should EU countries support a UN Framework Convention on International Tax Cooperation. *Intertax, 52*(5), 358.

Fung, S. (2017). The questionable legitimacy of the OECD/G20 BEPS Project. *Erasmus Law Review, 10*(2), 76. https://doi.org/10.5553/ELR.000085

Ganghof, S. (2006). *The politics of income taxation: A comparative analysis of advanced industrial countries*. ECPR Press.

Genschel, P. (2002). Globalization, tax competition and the welfare state. *Policy & Society, 30*(2), 245.

[29] United Nations General Assembly (UNGA) (2023a), paras 33, 39.

[30] United Nations General Assembly (UNGA) (2023a), paras 42–3.

Gonzalez-Barreda, P. H. (2018). A historical analysis of the BEPS action plan: Old acquaintances, new friends and the need for a new approach. *Intertax, 46*(4), 278.
Graetz, M. J. (2001). Taxing international income: Inadequate principles, outdated concepts, and unsatisfactory policies. *Brooklyn Journal of International Law*, *26*(4), 1357, 1363.
Haque, N. (2023). *Digital services tax and the inclusive framework: The journey so far* (Vol. 5). City Law Review.
Harpaz, A. (2023). International tax reform: Who gets a seat at the table? *University of Pennsylvania Journal of International Law, 44(4)*, 1007.
Herzfeld, M. (2017). The case against BEPS: Lessons for tax coordination. *Florida Tax Review, 21*(1), 1, 29–36.
Jimenez, A. M. (2018). BEPS, the digital(ized) economy and the taxation of services and royalties. *Intertax, 46*(8), 620.
OECD. (2017a). *Multilateral Convention to Implement Tax Treaty Related Measures to Prevent Base Erosion And Profit Shifting* (No. OECD/LEGAL/0432; p. Article 19). https://www.oecd.org/tax/treaties/multilateral-convention-to-implement-tax-treaty-related-measures-to-prevent-BEPS.htm
OECD. (2017b). *UN Model Tax Convention on Income and on Capital: Condensed Version 2017*. Organisation for Economic Cooperation and Development.
Oei, S.-Y. (2022). World tax policy in the world tax polity? An event history analysis of OECD/G20 BEPS Inclusive Framework Membership. *Yale Journal of International Law, 47*, 199.
Ozai, I. (2020). Institutional and structural legitimacy deficits in the international tax regime. *World Tax Journal, 12*(1), 53–54.
Ozai, I. (2025). Global justice in the reshaping of international tax. *Journal of International Economic Law, 27*(639), 642.
Peters, C. (2015). Developing countries' reactions to the G20/OECD action plan on base erosion and profit shifting. *Bulletin for International Taxation, 69*(6–7).
Rocha, S. A. (2017). The other side of BEPS: "Imperial Taxation" and "International Tax Imperialism." In A. Christians & S. A. Rocha (Eds.), *Tax sovereignty in the BEPS era* (pp. 179, 190–196, para 9.04). Wolters Kluwer.
Roelofsen, A. (2024). Ontwikkelingen in de internationale belastingarena. *Weekblad Fiskaal Recht, 110*, 9–18.
Rosenzweig, A. H. (2015). Defining a country's "fair share" of taxes. *Florida State University Law Review, 42*(2), 373.
United Nations. (2022). *Promotion of Inclusive and effective International Tax Cooperation at the United Nations: Nigeria revised draft resolution* (No. UN Doc A/C.2/77/L.11/Rev.1). United Nations General Assembly.
United Nations. (2023a). *Co-Coordinators' Report* (No. UN Doc E/C.18/2023/CRP.40). United Nations Committee of Experts on International Cooperation in Tax Matters.
United Nations. (2023b). *Resolution 77/244: Promotion of inclusive and effective International Tax Cooperation at the United Nations* (No. UN Doc A/RES/77/244). United Nations General Assembly.
Inputs to the First Session: United Nations Ad Hoc Committee to Draft Terms of Reference for a United Nations Framework Convention on International Tax Cooperation. https://financing.desa.un.org/un-tax-convention/first-session
Inputs to the Second Session: United Nations Committee to Draft Terms of Reference for a United Nations Framework Convention on International Tax Cooperation. https://financing.desa.un.org/un-tax-convention/second-session
United Nations General Assembly (UNGA). (2023a). *Promotion of inclusive and effective International Tax Cooperation at the United Nations: Report of the Secretary-General 78/235 (SG Report)* (No. UN Doc A/78/235).
United Nations General Assembly (UNGA). (2023b). *Resolution 78/230: Promotion of inclusive and effective International Tax Cooperation at the United Nations* (No. UN Doc A/RES/78/230). United Nations General Assembly.

United Nations General Assembly (UNGA). (2024). *Chair's proposal for draft terms of reference (TOR)* (No. UN Doc A/AC.295/2024/L.4.).

Vogel, K. (1988). Worldwide vs. Source Taxation of Income – A review and re-evaluation of arguments (Part I). *Intertax, 16*(8), 216.

Chapter 4
The Objectives of the Framework Tax Convention

Abstract The objectives of the FTC as set out in the UNGA resolution 79/235 are to foster inclusive, effective tax cooperation; establish responsive governance; and build an equitable international tax system for sustainable development. This chapter analyses inclusivity, governance structures, and sustainable development's role as a guiding principle, linking it to legitimacy, domestic resource mobilisation, and alignment with human rights obligations in reshaping tax norms.

Framework Conventions typically commence with a concise statement of their objectives,[1] often termed an 'overarching objective', 'ultimate objective',[2] or a goal that parties aspire to achieve.[3] The objectives of the FTC were a focal point of deliberations within the Ad Hoc Committee, culminating in Article 7 of the TOR. This article delineates three core components, reflecting a comprehensive approach:[4]

FTC should include a clear statement of its objectives. In that regard, it should:

---

[1] WHO Framework Convention on Tobacco Control (adopted 21 May 2003, entered into force 27 February 2005) 2302 UNTS 166 (FCTC) art 3: 'The objective of this Convention and its protocols is to protect present and future generations from the devastating health, social, environmental and economic consequences of tobacco consumption and exposure to tobacco smoke by providing a framework for tobacco control measures to be implemented by the Parties at the national, regional and international levels in order to reduce continually and substantially the prevalence of tobacco use and exposure to tobacco smoke'. It is not clear if this is the same as the 'object and purpose of a treaty' in the sense of the Vienna Convention on the Law of Treaties (signed 23 May 1969, entered into force 27 January 1980) 1155 UNTS 331 (VCLT) art 18, 31(1).

[2] UNFCCC (n 39 in Chap. 2) art 2: 'The ultimate objective of this Convention and any related legal instruments that the Conference of the Parties may adopt is to achieve, in accordance with the relevant provisions of the Convention, stabilization of greenhouse gas concentrations in the atmosphere at a level that would prevent dangerous anthropogenic interference with the climate system. Such a level should be achieved within a time-frame sufficient to allow ecosystems to adapt naturally to climate change, to ensure that food production is not threatened and to enable economic development to proceed in a sustainable manner'.

[3] Convention on Long-Range Transboundary Air Pollution (signed 13 November 1979, entered into force 16 March 1983) 1302 UNTS 217 (CLRTAP) art 2.

[4] United Nations General Assembly (UNGA) (2024), para 7.

E. Vanderbruggen, *Reconstructing Global Tax Governance*, SpringerBriefs in Law, https://doi.org/10.1007/978-981-95-5617-5_4

(a) Establish fully inclusive and effective international tax cooperation in terms of substance and process;
(b) Establish a system of governance for international tax cooperation capable of responding to existing and future tax and tax-related challenges on an ongoing basis;
(c) Establish an inclusive, fair, transparent, efficient, equitable and effective international tax system for sustainable development, with a view to enhancing the legitimacy, certainty, resilience and fairness of international tax rules, while addressing challenges to strengthening DRM.[5]

4.1 'Inclusive and Effective'

The first-listed objective of the FTC is to 'establish fully inclusive and effective international tax cooperation in terms of substance and process'. Initially, the Zero Draft TOR proposed 'to set out fundamental principles', but this was amended during the Second Session to 'to establish', following proposals from the African Group, among others.[6]

According to the SG Report, 'inclusive and effective in terms of substance' encompasses a range of issues, notably that international tax rules should bolster LMICs' capacity to finance their Sustainable Development Goals (SDGs).[7] Inclusivity and effectiveness also pertain to the ability of LMICs to implement international tax rules, which hinges on capacity building and the adoption of simple and stable regulatory frameworks.[8]

The efficacy of international tax cooperation under the FTC is contingent upon the availability of adequate resources, particularly the substantial resources required to support the Secretariat's operations.[9]

---

[5] Ibid.

[6] According to the Secretary-General's Report, 'inclusive and effective in terms of substance' encompasses a range of issues, notably that international tax rules should bolster developing states' capacity to finance their Sustainable Development Goals (SDGs). Inclusivity and effectiveness also pertain to the ability of developing countries to implement international tax rules, which hinges on capacity building and the adoption of simple and stable regulatory frameworks. The efficacy of international tax cooperation under the FTC is contingent upon the availability of adequate resources, particularly the substantial resources required to support the Secretariat's operations. African Group, Inputs to the Second Session (n 44 in Chap. 2).

[7] United Nations General Assembly (UNGA) (2023), paras 10–8.

[8] United Nations General Assembly (UNGA) (2023), para 12; Burgers and Mosquera Valderrama (2017), pp. 29, 32.

[9] United Nations General Assembly (UNGA) (2023) addresses how the Secretariat will be financed.

4.2 'Establish a System of Governance'

The second component of the objective addresses the governance structure, stipulating: 'Establish a system of governance for international tax cooperation capable of responding to existing and emerging tax and tax-related challenges on an ongoing basis.' This entails the creation of a robust framework comprising bodies, subsidiary bodies, and defined rules and procedures. Such a structure is intended to operate continuously and possess the requisite capacity and adaptability to address both current and future tax-related challenges effectively.

According to the SG Report, 'in terms of process' denotes the provision of meaningful opportunities for all countries, particularly LMICs, to participate actively in the development of international tax rules. This includes involvement in agenda-setting, decision-making, monitoring, and dispute resolution.[10] To facilitate this, adequate resources must be allocated to enable LMICs to attend meetings and access capacity-building support where necessary. Furthermore, sufficient time must be allocated to allow all countries, including those with limited experience or smaller delegations, to thoroughly evaluate proposed rules.

4.3 'Establish an International Tax System'

It seems the most ambitious articulation of the objective is comprised in paragraph (c) of Art. 7 of the TOR. While subparagraphs (a) and (b) refer to international tax cooperation, paragraph (c) sets out that the objective is to 'establish an international tax system,' a term that seems to transcend mere cooperation. Paragraph (c) connects several significant principles as attributes for the international tax system, including fairness or equity, inclusivity, efficiency and effectiveness, transparency many of which were recalled in the SG Report and in UNGA Resolutions 77/244 and 78/230. The central purpose for the international tax system is 'sustainable development', while 'enhancing the legitimacy, certainty, resilience, and fairness of international tax rules, and addressing challenges to DRM'.

As articulated in Resolutions 78/230, this objective requires 'scaling up international tax cooperation by establishing the legal basis for fully inclusive and more effective international tax cooperation in terms of substance and process'. To achieve this, the international tax system envisioned by the FTC must encompass principles, rules, bodies, and procedures designed to facilitate cooperation in addressing tax and tax-related challenges.

[10] United Nations General Assembly (UNGA) (2023), para 11.

4.4 'An International Tax System for Sustainable Development'

Sustainable development, a 'widely accepted objective of the global community', is uniquely positioned within the FTC, explicitly incorporated into its objectives, principles, and commitments.[11]

As will be examined in more detail below,[12] although sustainable development is originally rooted in environmental conservation and resource preservation,[13] its scope extends to broader aspirations. For example, while the World Trade Organization (WTO) preamble in 1995 linked sustainable development to resource conservation, subsequent references have treated it as an wider concept.[14] Sustainable development is enshrined in numerous binding international treaties and is the subject of declarations, recommendations, and standards by international organisations.[15] In 2002, the International Law Association (ILA) Committee on the Legal Aspects of Sustainable Development drafted the New Delhi Declaration on the Principles of International Law Related to Sustainable Development.[16] This declaration delineates seven principles: the duty of states to steward natural resources,[17] equity and poverty eradication, the principle of common but differentiated responsibilities, human health, public participation and access to justice, good governance,[18] and the integration of social (including human rights), economic, and environmental objectives. In its 1997 judgment, the International Court of Justice (ICJ) acknowledged that 'the need to reconcile economic development with environmental protection is aptly expressed in the concept of sustainable development',[19] yet refrained

---

[11] Gehring and Newcombe (2011), p. 3; see also International Court of Justice (ICJ) (2025) (ICJ AO), para 147.

[12] See below Sect. 7.2.

[13] Brundtland (1987), p. ix (*Brundtland Report*).

[14] Marrakesh Agreement establishing the World Trade Organization (adopted 15 April 1994, entered into force 1 January 1995) 1867 UNTS 154 Preamble: 'While allowing for the optimal use of the world's resources in accordance with the objective of sustainable development, seeking both to protect and preserve the environment and to enhance the means for doing so in a manner consistent with their respective needs and concerns at different levels of economic development'; World Trade Organization (WTO) (1998): 'We shall also continue to improve our efforts towards the objectives of sustained economic growth and sustainable development'.

[15] Cordonier Segger and Khalfan (2004), pp. 32–36.

[16] International Law Association (ILA) (2002) (New Delhi Declaration).

[17] United Nations (1992) (Rio de Janeiro, 3 June–14 June 1992) (12 August 1992) UN Doc A/CONF.151/26 (Rio Declaration) Principle 23.

[18] United Nations (2002); 'Report of the World Summit on Sustainable Development' UN Doc A/CONF.199/20 (2002) annex 'Plan of Implementation of the World Summit on Sustainable Development' (Johannesburg Plan of Implementation), para 4.

[19] *Gabčíkovo-Nagymaros Project (Hungary v Slovakia)* (Merits) [1997] ICJ Rep 7, 78 (*Gabčíkovo-Nagymaros*), para 140.

from endorsing its discrete normative or regulatory status.[20] In the 2025 ICJ Advisory Opinion (AO) on Climate Change, the Court referred to sustainable development as a legal principle rather than a concept, and part of the applicable law in relation to climate change. While the ICJ confirmed that this legal principle guides the interpretation of conventional norms and the identification of customs, assigning normative content to sustainable development in and of itself may prove challenging, as, despite widespread agreement among states that development should be sustainable, consensus on the means to achieve this—except in extreme circumstances—often remains elusive.[21] This challenge is likely to persist in the realm of international taxation.

The nexus between achieving SDGs and addressing national and international tax challenges, particularly in LMICs with limited fiscal resources, was a recurrent theme before the Ad Hoc Committee.[22]

The FTC aims to establish a fairer and more equitable international tax system to promote greater equity between HICs and LMICs, with sustainable development as a core objective. This system, and the cooperation it entails, must be inclusive and oriented towards sustainable development. Its rules should be designed to enhance countries' capacities to achieve their SDGs, while remaining resilient and adaptable to address future challenges and evolving circumstances.

4.5 Fair and Equitable International Tax Rules

Fairness or equity are central principles to the proposed FTC. Its objective includes establishing an inclusive international tax system that is, among other things, 'fair' and 'equitable' with a view of 'enhancing the fairness of international tax rules'. Fairness is reaffirmed in the FTC's principles which include ensuring 'sufficient flexibility to ensure equitable results as societies and technology evolve, and ensures 'fairness in allocation of international taxing rights'. The principle is furthermore repeated in the commitments, as Resolution 79/235 prescribes 'equitable taxation of multinational enterprises'.

The possible implications of proposing fairness or equity as foundational principles for the international tax system are discussed in more detail in below Chap. 7.[23]

---

[20] Orakhelashvili (2022), p. 426.

[21] Boyle et al. (2021), p. 125; ICJ AO (n 11 in this chapter), para 147.

[22] For example, see India, 1st Meeting of the First Session (26 April 2024) (n 44 in Chap. 2): 'India is of the strong view that effective international tax cooperation is a critical element in meeting the requirements for attaining the sustainable development goals of member states who are at different stages of development'.

[23] See Sect. 7.3.

4.6 Domestic Resource Mobilisation

The objective of the FTC encompasses international cooperation to enhance DRM. Although DRM is not explicitly referenced elsewhere in the TOR, to the disappointment of HICs, it is closely intertwined with other FTC principles, such as achieving sustainable development, ensuring transparency and accountability of taxpayers, and addressing commitments like combating tax evasion by high-net-worth individuals and tax-related IFFs.

The Addis Ababa Action Agenda underscores the necessity of additional domestic resources to achieve sustainable development.[24] Furthermore, Resolution 78/230 explicitly references DRM and directed the Ad Hoc Committee to consider it during the drafting of the TOR.

During Ad Hoc Committee discussions, HICs repeatedly argued that enhancing the international allocation of taxing rights in favour of LMICs would have limited impact. This stance countered the insistence of LMICs that the FTC address inequities in international taxing rights. Instead, HICs urged LMICs to prioritise reforms to their national tax systems, addressing issues such as lack of transparency, narrow tax bases, and insufficient administrative capacity.[25] A pertinent question emerges: whether it is equitable to allocate greater tax revenues to LMICs to support their development goals in all circumstances, for example even if national tax systems allow wealthy and influential elites within those countries to remain undertaxed. The EU, in a joint statement, alongside Germany,[26] advocated for embedding DRM, capacity building, and tax compliance as commitments within the FTC.[27] Singapore proposed establishing DRM as the subject of an early protocol.[28]

The United States critiqued the Zero Draft TOR for insufficient emphasis on DRM, arguing that its inclusion within an objective 'mentions [DRM] in such a way that little importance is placed on it'.[29] This criticism is not wholly substantiated, as several commitments in the TOR—such as those addressing tax avoidance, evasion, and IFFs—and proposed subjects for early protocols, including taxation of high-net-worth individuals and IFFs, are directly relevant to DRM.

Given the primary motivations driving LMICs' advocacy for the FTC, the absence of more explicit references to DRM is unsurprising. LMICs frequently

---

[24] United Nations (2015), para 22.

[25] 6th Meeting of the First Session (30 April 2024) (n 44 in Chap. 2). See also International Monetary Fund (IMF) (2024) (G20 Note), which discusses curtailing tax incentives, VAT, excise, reducing informality and non-compliance, base broadening, administration and transparency. The G20 Note also calculates that the potential revenue yield from domestic tax reform options is estimated to be eight times higher than that from international tax cooperation measures: at 36.

[26] Germany, Inputs to the Second Session (n 44 in Chap. 2).

[27] See the statement dated 29 July 2024 by the European Union, proposing that commitments should be on a complementary basis: European Union, Inputs to the Second Session (n 44 in Chap. 2).

[28] Singapore, Inputs to the Second Session (n 44 in Chap. 2) point 4.2.

[29] United States, Inputs to the Second Session (n 44 in Chap. 2) 3.

redirected discussions towards international taxing rights when confronted with domestic tax challenges, suggesting a reluctance to include prioritising improvements in domestic tax administration and international assistance.[30]

Case Law

Gabčíkovo-Nagymaros Project (Hungary v Slovakia), ICJ Reports 7 (1997).

References

Boyle, A. E., Redgwell, C., & Birnie, P. W. (2021). *International law and the environment* (4th ed.). Oxford University Press.

Brundtland, G. H. (1987). *Our common future: The World Commission on Environment and Development*. Oxford University Press.

Burgers, I., & Mosquera Valderrama, I. J. (2017). Corporate taxation and BEPS: A fair slice for developing countries? *Erasmus Law Review*, *10*(1), 29, 32.

Cordonier Segger, M.-C., & Khalfan, A. (2004). *Sustainable development law: Principles, practices and prospects*. Oxford University Press.

Gehring, M. W., & Newcombe, A. (2011). Chapter 1: An introduction to sustainable development in world investment law. In M.-C. Cordonier Segger, M. W. Gehring, & A. P. Newcombe (Eds.), *Sustainable development in world investment law* (p. 3). Kluwer Law International.

International Court of Justice (ICJ). (2025, July 23). *Obligations of States in respect of climate change (ICJ AO)*. Retrieved July 27, 2025, from https://www.icj-cij.org/sites/default/files/case-related/187/187-20250723-adv-01-00-en.pdf

International Law Association (ILA). (2002). *New Delhi Declaration of Principles of International Law Relating to Sustainable Development* (No. Report of the Seventieth Conference).

International Monetary Fund (IMF). (2024). *G20 note on alternative options for revenue mobilization* (pp. 28–35). Retrieved July 22, 2025, from https://www.imf.org/external/np/g20/062424.htm

Orakhelashvili, A. (2022). *Akehurst's modern introduction to international law* (9th ed.). Routledge.

United Nations. (1992). *Rio Declaration on Environment and Development* (No. UN Doc A/CONF.151/26). UN Conference on Environment and Development.

United Nations. (2002). *Plan of implementation of the World Summit on Sustainable Development* (No. UN Doc A/CONF.199/20 (Annex); p. para 4).

United Nations. (2015). *Resolution 69/313: Addis Ababa Action Agenda of the third international conference on financing for development* (No. UN Doc A/RES/69/313). United Nations. https://www.un.org/esa/ffd/wp-content/uploads/2015/08/AAAA_Outcome.pdf

Inputs to the First Session: United Nations Ad Hoc Committee to Draft Terms of Reference for a United Nations Framework Convention on International Tax Cooperation. https://financing.desa.un.org/un-tax-convention/first-session

Inputs to the Second Session: United Nations Committee to Draft Terms of Reference for a United Nations Framework Convention on International Tax Cooperation. https://financing.desa.un.org/un-tax-convention/second-session

[30] India, 4th Meeting of the First Session (29 April 2024) (n 44 in Chap. 2).

United Nations General Assembly (UNGA). (2023). *Promotion of inclusive and effective international tax cooperation at the United Nations: Report of the Secretary-General 78/235 (SG Report)* (No. UN Doc A/78/235).
United Nations General Assembly (UNGA). (2024). *Chair's Proposal for Draft Terms of Reference (TOR)* (No. UN Doc A/AC.295/2024/L.4.).
World Trade Organization (WTO). (1998). *Ministerial Declaration* (No. WTO Doc WT/MIN(98)/DEC/1; p. para 4).

Chapter 5
Principles of the Framework Tax Convention

Abstract This chapter explores the nine guiding principles of the UN Framework Convention on International Tax Cooperation (FTC), including inclusivity, equity and fairness, sovereignty, human rights alignment, and sustainable development. It analyses how these principles aim to create an inclusive, equitable, and adaptable international tax system, recognizing LMIC needs. The chapter evaluates their role in shaping tax governance, fostering fairness in taxing rights, and addressing challenges like tax evasion and digital economy taxation, while ensuring flexibility for evolving global tax landscapes.

A framework convention lists fundamental guiding ideas that parties of the FTC use as a reference to achieve objectives. These principles are part of the binding treaty, but not binding like rules because of the language used. The principles of the FTC guide parties on how to achieve the objectives and create future obligations. They do not determine what rules to create in the future. The parties of the FTC are bound to consider the principles if they believe them relevant to the issue. For the FTC, the list of principles is relevant and important, but it is difficult to predict their impact on future rulemaking.[1]

As was already mentioned above,[2] the TOR lists nine principles in Article 9—a) to i) below. Some are related to the objectives of the TOR.

[1] Bodansky (1999), p. 19.

[2] See above Sect. 1.3.

E. Vanderbruggen, *Reconstructing Global Tax Governance*, SpringerBriefs in Law, https://doi.org/10.1007/978-981-95-5617-5_5

5.1 'Be Universal in Approach and Scope and Fully Consider the Different Needs, Priorities, and Capacities of All Countries, Including Developing Countries, in Particular Countries in Special Situations'

Resolution 78/230 mandates consideration of the diverse needs, priorities, and capacities of LMICs.[3] The SG Report critiques the OECD's Pillar Two and the Global Forum for their lack of alignment with the capacities and priorities of LMICs.[4]

This principle of differentiation entails that parties to the same treaty regime may not bear identical responsibilities and obligations, but rather those tailored to the specific circumstances and capacities of each state or group of states. In this context, treaty regimes may assign less onerous obligations to LMICs, acknowledging their resource and capacity constraints.[5]

The FTC incorporates this principle. As China stated, 'our framework must be sufficiently flexible to acknowledge the diversity of Members. We must ensure that responsibilities imposed on countries are equitable and account for their varying capacities and circumstances.'[6]

By embedding this principle, the TOR introduces the notion that commitments under the FTC may differ between LMICs and HICs. Such differentiation could shape international tax cooperation obligations. The SG Report highlights this need in relation to the Global Forum, noting that 'it can be difficult for many developing countries to comply with the reciprocity requirements'.[7] Consequently, a future protocol might establish an exchange of information regime with less burdensome implementation obligations for LMICs.[8] Another pertinent example is the Global Minimum Tax, where the uniform application of a 15% tax rate has been critiqued

[3] United Nations General Assembly (UNGA) (2023b), point 6(a): 'To take into account the needs, priorities and capacities of all countries, in particular, developing countries.'

[4] United Nations General Assembly (UNGA) (2023a), paras 39–42.

[5] In 1947, the General Agreement on Tariffs and Trade already recognized the disadvantaged position of LMICs, that 'the developed contracting parties do not expect reciprocity for commitments made by them in trade negotiations to reduce or remove tariffs and other barriers to the trade of less-developed contracting parties': General Agreement on Tariffs and Trade (signed 30 October 1947, entered into force 1 January 1948) 55 UNTS 194 (GATT) art XXXVI(8). However, another framework convention, the UNFCCC (n 39 in Chap. 2), is often cited as the best illustration of the concept of differentiation in Principle 7 of the Rio Declaration (United Nations, 1992): 'The developed countries acknowledge the responsibility that they bear in the international pursuit of sustainable development in view of the pressures their societies place on the global environment and of the technologies and financial resources they command'.

[6] China, 4th Meeting of the First Session (29 April 2024) (n 44 in Chap. 2).

[7] United Nations General Assembly (UNGA) (2023a), para 39.

[8] As the Tax Justice Network suggested at the First Session of the Ad Hoc Committee, some low-income countries can enjoy the benefit of receiving international information even while their own information collection is not yet fully operational: Tax Justice Network, Inputs to the First Session (n 44 in Chap. 2) 7.

as challenging.[9] Some states may seek differentiated approaches, potentially retaining greater flexibility to offer tax incentives than others.

Differentiation of obligations is a familiar feature in environmental agreements, following its articulation in the 1992 Rio Declaration and the FCCC as the principle of Common But Differentiated Responsibilities and Respective Capabilities (within National Circumstances) (CBDR-RC).[10]

5.2 'Recognize that Every Member State Has the Sovereign Right to Decide Its Tax Policies and Practices, While Also Respecting the Sovereignty of Other Member States'

From the perspective of customary international law and jurisdiction, the power to tax constitutes a fundamental element of state sovereignty,[11] which the Secretary-General's Report adopted as a foundation for its analysis.[12] The concept of tax sovereignty was a recurring theme during the Ad Hoc Committee's deliberations.[13] The United States underscored the importance of preserving national sovereignty in international tax cooperation,[14] stating: 'Addressing base erosion and profit shifting is crucial, but we must ensure that it does not encroach upon the sovereignty of nations in determining their own tax policies'.[15] Japan echoed this view, asserting: 'Taxation is inherently a matter of sovereignty, and each state retains the right to establish its tax policies and decide whether to adopt new international tax rules'.[16] Similarly, China highlighted sovereignty in the context of enforcement, noting: 'International cooperation in tax enforcement is vital, but it must respect the

[9] de la Feria (2024), p. 58.

[10] Rio Declaration (United Nations, 1992), Principle 7; UNFCCC (n 39 in Chap. 2) art 3(1); Paris Agreement (signed 22 April 2016, entered into force 4 November 2016) 3156 UNTS 79 (Paris Agreement) art 2(2). See also International Court of Justice (ICJ) (2025).

[11] Vanderbruggen (2001), p. 115.

[12] Report (n 19 in Chap. 1), para 1: 'A country's domestic tax system reflects its values and national priorities and is a fundamental aspect of its exercise of national sovereignty [...] [T]he international tax system should reflect universal values, including the principle of sovereign equality of all Member States'.

[13] United Kingdom, 2nd Meeting of the First Session (26 April 2024) (n 44 in Chap. 2); Republic of Korea, 2nd Meeting of the First Session (26 April 2024) (n 44 in Chap. 2); United States, 4th Meeting of the First Session (29 April 2024) (n 44 in Chap. 2); Japan, 1st Meeting of the First Session (26 April 2024) (n 44 in Chap. 2).

[14] United States, 4th Meeting of the First Session (29 April 2024) (n 44 in Chap. 2): 'As we work towards greater international cooperation, we must never lose sight of the importance of national sovereignty. Each country must retain the right to make decisions that reflect its own economic and social priorities'.

[15] United States, 2nd Meeting of the First Session (26 April 2024) (n 44 in Chap. 2).

[16] Japan, 1st Meeting of the First Session (26 April 2024) (n 44 in Chap. 2).

sovereignty of nations. Our enforcement mechanisms should support, not supplant, national efforts.'[17]

The Zero Draft TOR, prepared by the Chair of the Ad Hoc Committee, articulated the principle of sovereignty as follows:

> Recognise that every Member State possesses the sovereign right to determine the policies and practices of its domestic tax system, while bearing the responsibility to ensure that such policies and practices do not undermine the effectiveness of the tax base or system of other Member States.[18]

This formulation, which was adjusted in the final text, acknowledged that, under international law, states are entitled to formulate their own tax rules, encompassing not only tax incentives and competition but also measures to counter BEPS and tax avoidance. Consequently, if a state enacts policies to counteract another state's tax exemptions on the grounds of 'harmful tax competition', the legality of those exemptions under international law is implicitly affirmed.

Incorporating the principle of tax sovereignty into the FTC serves primarily to moderate the application and interpretation of existing commitments and future rulemaking. States may invoke tax sovereignty within the FTC framework to justify reluctance to adopt specific commitments or participate in certain forms of international cooperation.

As this author has argued elsewhere, it is doubtful that fiscal sovereignty somehow justifies a differential treatment than other areas of state regulation.[19] The argument that tax (and thus tax sovereignty) provides the means to many other needs of the State, does not change that the concept of sovereignty as the supreme authority within a territory does not leave any room for a 'more supreme' sovereignty for tax than other fields.[20] Even practically, it is not persuasive that states' policies on taxation are somehow more important than those that directly impact human life such as policy regarding human rights, public health, the environment or security. The need to re-evaluate the boundaries of Westphalian fiscal sovereignty is today more compelling than ever before.[21]

---

[17] China, 15th Meeting of the First Session (7 May 2024) (n 44 in Chap. 2).

[18] United Nations Department of Economic and Social Affairs (UNDESA) (2024), para 9. However, Singapore proposed to cut this language: Singapore Inputs to the Second Session (n 44 in Chap. 2) point 1.

[19] Vanderbruggen (2025), pp. 114, 135.

[20] Salacuse (2021), p. 481 (arguing that 'the power to tax is fundamental to the power to govern since it provides governments with the necessary means to carry out their governmental functions'); Besson (2012), p. 366, para 1; Carrillo-Salcedo (1996), p. 44.

[21] Dietsch (2015), p. 2107.

5.3 'In the Pursuit of International Tax Cooperation to Align with States' Obligations Under International Human Rights Law'

The Ad Hoc Committee endorsed the inclusion of a principle within the FTC referencing international human rights law. It was observed that 'the obligations undertaken by states upon ratifying human rights treaties are frequently overlooked in international tax cooperation',[22] a point not originally addressed in Resolution 78/230 or the SG Report.

Incorporating a principle grounded in international human rights law could significantly influence international tax cooperation, given the manifold intersections between human rights and taxation. During the Ad Hoc Committee's discussions, several pertinent issues were raised, including the right to privacy and the exchange of information.[23] The significance of the TOR's invocation of respect for human rights is discussed in detail below in Chap. 7.[24]

5.4 'Take a Holistic, Sustainable Development Perspective that Covers in a Balanced and Integrated Manner Economic, Social and Environmental Policy Aspects'

As previously outlined, the objective of the FTC, as articulated in the TOR, is to establish a fairer and more equitable international tax system to promote parity between HICs and LMICs while advancing sustainable development. This principle reaffirms that objective.

The SG Report highlighted that LMICs advocated for a broader approach to tax cooperation, extending beyond trade and investment to encompass socio-economic, health, environmental, and gender equality considerations.[25] Prior to the Ad Hoc Committee's formulation of the TOR, Resolution 78/230 explicitly included financing the SDGs as a core component of the FTC.[26]

---

[22] Centre for Economic and Social Rights, Inputs to the First Session (n 44 in Chap. 2) 4. See also Tax Justice Network Africa, Inputs to the Second Session (n 44 in Chap. 2) 2–3.

[23] Ibid.

[24] Please refer below to Sect. 7.4.

[25] United Nations General Assembly (UNGA) (2023a), para 5. For recent outcomes of the Economic and Social Council forum on financing for development follow-up, see <https://financing.desa.un.org/what-we-do/ECOSOC/financing-development-forum/outcomes>. For information on the special meeting of the Council on international cooperation in tax matters, see <https://financing.desa.un.org/ecosoc-special-meetings>. For information on the Group of 20 High-level Tax Symposium, see <www.g20.org/en/about-g20/#previous-summits>.

[26] United Nations General Assembly (UNGA) (2023b), p. 2. See also point 6(b), which requests the ad hoc intergovernmental committee, in elaborating the draft terms of reference for a framework

This principle directs FTC parties to pursue 'equitable, effective, and inclusive' cooperation through a comprehensive lens, incorporating socio-economic, health, and environmental dimensions.

One prominent application of this principle, discussed at the Ad Hoc Committee, pertains to environmental taxation. Both HICs and LMICs, including Norway,[27] Germany,[28] and Brazil, underscored the potential of carbon and other environmental taxes. Brazil noted: 'Environmental taxes offer a unique opportunity to align revenue generation with our sustainable development goals. By taxing environmentally harmful activities, we can raise revenue while safeguarding our planet.'[29] During the sixth meeting, environmental taxation was identified as an innovative approach to DRM that aligns with SDG objectives. Delegates further emphasised the need for capacity building in environmental taxation to equip LMICs with the expertise to design and implement effective policies. The TOR also designated tax cooperation on environmental challenges as a potential subject for a future protocol.

5.5 'Be Sufficiently Flexible, Resilient and Agile to Ensure Equitable and Effective Results as Societies, Technology and Business Models and the International Tax Cooperation Landscapes Evolve'

The United Nations General Assembly directed the Ad Hoc Committee to address 'the need for sufficient flexibility and resilience in the international tax system to ensure equitable outcomes as technology, business models, and the international tax cooperation landscape evolve'.[30]

This principle is obviously closely linked to the challenges posed by the digital economy as addressed by BEPS Pillar I and anticipates future technological advancements that could impact states' tax positions. It seeks to guide the parties to the FTC in ensuring that the international tax system remains equitable despite technological and other developments. As articulated by the Chair: 'The digital and gig economies are transforming our world, yet our tax systems have struggled to adapt. We must collaborate to ensure that these sectors contribute equitably to our economies, leaving no one excluded from this digital transformation'.[31] The subject

convention, as follows: 'b) to take a holistic, sustainable development perspective that considers interactions with other important economic, social and environmental policy areas'.

[27] In its written inputs to the First Session (n 44 in Chap. 2), Norway referred to opportunities for cooperation on taxes related to climate change and the environment.

[28] Singapore, 6th Meeting of the First Session (n 44 in Chap. 2).

[29] Brazil, 6th Meeting of the First Session (n 44 in Chap. 2).

[30] United Nations General Assembly (UNGA) (2023b), point 6(c).

[31] Chair opening remarks, 14th Meeting of the First Session (6 May 2024) (n 44 in Chap. 2).

matter also intersects with the first of the Protocols, which will encompass digital services.

5.6 'Contribute to Achieving Sustainable Development by Ensuring Fairness in the Allocation of Taxing Rights Under the International Tax System'

This principle is designed to support the establishment of a fairer and more equitable international tax system, fostering greater parity between HICs and LMICs while advancing sustainable development. Its emphasis lies on the allocation of taxing rights. Although no UN Members would advocate for an inherently unfair international tax system, the terms 'equitable' and 'fair' alone do not inherently generate normative content. Nonetheless, enshrining a principle that underscores the fairness of taxing rights is potentially significant. It obliges Members to evaluate subsequent commitments through this lens, thereby influencing the progressive development of international tax law to align more closely with other domains of international law, including environmental, developmental, trade, and investment frameworks. The implications of the FTC's reference to fairness in connection with international taxing rights is examined in more detail in Chap. 7.[32]

5.7 'Provide for Rules that Are as Simple and Easy to Administer as the Subject Matter Allows'

The complexity of certain international tax rules and guidance, often developed by the OECD, has been repeatedly highlighted by LMICs and noted in the SG Report,[33] which states: 'International tax rules need to be as simple and easy to administer as the subject allows.' This principle is closely tied to the effectiveness of implementation and the need for capacity building in LMICs.

Scholarly literature has underscored that tax measures designed primarily for HICs may not align with the circumstances and resources of LMICs. For instance, Annet Wanyana Oguttu, examining the BEPS reforms introduced through the MLI, observed that hybrid mismatches present a complex challenge for LMICs.[34] Nevertheless, Oguttu advocates for LMICs to adopt these provisions, as articulated in her work. Similarly, Charles Irish has highlighted disparities in transfer pricing contexts between HICs and LMICs.[35]

---

[32] See below Sect. 7.3.

[33] United Nations General Assembly (UNGA) (2023a), para 12; See also Reeves (2022).

[34] Oguttu (2017), p. 220.

[35] Irish (1986), p. 91.

5.8 'Ensure Certainty for Taxpayers and Governments'

The SG Report underscored the necessity for 'sufficient stability to enable businesses to plan effectively for the long term'.[36] This principle directs states to prioritise predictability in the application of tax regimes, with significant implications for dispute resolution and the efficacy of implementation.

Enhancing legal certainty in tax matters constitutes a core policy priority for the OECD, G20, and the International Monetary Fund (IMF). Following an initial report in 2017[37] and a subsequent update in 2018,[38] G20 Leaders have consistently underscored their commitment to advancing tax certainty. The OECD's initiatives in this domain emphasise dispute prevention, the promotion of bilateral and multilateral approaches over unilateral measures, and the deployment of various tax certainty mechanisms. These include Mutual Agreement Procedures (MAPs), Advance Pricing Arrangements (APAs), the International Compliance Assurance Programme (ICAP), joint audits, and Country-by-Country Reporting (CbC Reporting). Within the OECD/G20/IMF framework, tax certainty encompasses a broad spectrum of considerations, including bolstering predictability in tax administration, particularly in LMICs, enhancing the transparency of tax dispute resolution mechanisms, and implementing tools such as APAs, joint tax audits, and measures to combat corruption.[39]

The OECD's efforts to enhance tax certainty address a broad spectrum of issues in tax policy and administration. In relation to the effective utilisation of CbC reports, the OECD Forum on Tax Administration (FTA), an initiative aimed at refining risk assessment and audit processes, has implemented several measures to support tax authorities. These include CbC report risk assessment workshops, the *Handbook on the Effective Use of CbC Reports in Tax Risk Assessment*, the Comparative Risk Assessment initiative (CoRA), and the Tax Risk Evaluation and Assurance Tool (TREAT). Additional OECD initiatives to reduce uncertainty in tax treaties encompass a range of measures, including the promotion of information exchange, the OECD International VAT/GST Guidelines, toolkits developed by the Platform for Collaboration on Tax, and the formulation of Medium-Term Revenue Strategies. Furthermore, the IMF provides extensive technical assistance in revenue mobilisation, encompassing tax policy design, legal drafting, and tax administration, while the joint OECD/UNDP Tax Inspectors Without Borders (TIWB) programme strengthens capacity in LMICs. The OECD has also initiated work exploring the nexus between tax morale and tax certainty, drawing on the 2017 tax certainty survey of businesses to foster discourse on attitudes towards tax compliance, particularly in LMICs. This includes examining the interplay between tax morale, integrity, and anti-corruption efforts, focusing on how corruption and

---

[36] Ibid.

[37] IMF and OECD (2017).

[38] IMF and OECD (2018).

[39] Pagone (2009); Demin (2020), p. 30; Elkins (2025), p. 40; Yusuf et al. (2024), p. 170.

integrity issues influence tax morale. Additionally, to ensure the clear and efficient administration of tax rules—a cornerstone of tax certainty—the OECD is enhancing its TPG and advancing the implementation of BEPS Actions 8–10 workstreams.

The OECD/G20/IMF framework identifies several practical tools to enhance tax certainty. Firstly, enhancing the clarity of tax legislation and increasing the predictability and consistency of tax administration are paramount. This entails reducing complexity and avoiding inappropriate retroactivity, while issuing rulings and technical interpretations promptly to foster taxpayer engagement and comprehension. Secondly, the OECD underscores that tax certainty is advanced through robust dispute prevention and resolution mechanisms. Dispute prevention tools enable taxpayers and tax authorities to address potential conflicts proactively, whereas dispute resolution mechanisms aim to settle disagreements expeditiously and equitably. Key among these is the implementation of systems to inform and support taxpayers in fulfilling their obligations, achieved through measures such as general rulings or other public statements by tax authorities, and mandatory publication of redacted private rulings and APAs to ensure transparency while safeguarding taxpayer privacy.[40] Thirdly, addressing tax uncertainty in the international context is critical, requiring the development and consistent implementation of international standards and guidance, simplification of treaty relief procedures, and utilisation of the BEPS MLI to expedite treaty amendments.

5.9 'Require Transparency and Accountability of All Taxpayers'

This principle pertains to combating tax evasion and avoidance, which the Addis Ababa Action Agenda links to the broader issue of IFFs.[41] In its opening remarks at the Ad Hoc Committee, Nigeria declared: 'Illicit financial flows constitute a severe impediment to our continent, depleting resources critically needed for development. We must adopt a resolute stance to ensure accountability for those engaged in such practices.'[42]

Civil society and the private sector are among the driving forces promoting enhanced transparency in tax matters. The 'B Team', a non-profit initiative established in 2013 by leaders from business and civil society to enhance corporate accountability by prioritising people, planet, and profit equitably,[43] issued a report in 2018 delineating its 'Responsible Tax Principles' (RTP). The RTP, developed

---

40 Thuronyi and Espejo (2013).

41 Addis Agenda (United Nations, 2015), para 23: 'We will redouble efforts to substantially reduce illicit financial flows by 2030, with a view to eventually eliminating them, including by combating tax evasion and corruption through strengthened national regulation and increased international cooperation'.

42 Nigeria, 13th Meeting of the First Session (6 May 2024) (n 44 in Chap. 2).

43 The B Team <https://www.bteam.org/> accessed 10 August 2025.

with contributions from leading companies, civil society, institutional investors, and representatives of international institutions, provide a robust framework for responsible tax practices in business. They have been endorsed and implemented by a founding group of companies.[44]

In the domain of tax management, RTP's referring to accountability, governance, compliance, and business structure mandate that tax oversight resides with the board of directors and that taxes are paid in alignment with the location of value creation. In the sphere of relationships with others, the RTP require businesses to collaborate with tax authorities to bolster effective tax systems, particularly by claiming tax incentives in a transparent and lawful manner. Transparency is a recurring theme across all RTP, notably in the area of stakeholder reporting, which obliges businesses to regularly disclose information to investors, policymakers, employees, civil society, and the public regarding their tax strategies and taxes paid.[45] In 2023, the 20 signatory companies of the RTP participated in an accountability exercise. The resulting report indicated strong performance against the RTP, achieving an average compliance rate of 93%. However, challenges persisted in implementing principles related to tax incentives and tax transparency.[46]

References

Besson, S. (2012). Sovereignty. In *Max Planck Encyclopedia of Public International Law* (p. 366, para 1).

Bodansky, D. (1999). *The Framework Convention/Protocol Approach* (No. Paper 1; Technical Briefing Series). World Health Organization (WHO). https://iris.who.int/handle/10665/65355

Carrillo-Salcedo, J.-A. (1996). *Droit Internationale et Souveraineté des États* (Vol. 257, p. 44). Receuil des Cours.

de la Feria, R. (2024). The perceived (un)fairness of the global minimum corporate tax rate. In W. Haslehner, G. Kofler, K. Pantazatou, & A. Rust (Eds.), *The Pillar 2 global minimum tax* (p. 58). Edward Elgar.

Demin, A. V. (2020). Certainty and uncertainty in tax law: Do opposites attract? *Legal-Economic Issues of Digital & Collaborative Economy, 9*(9), 30.

Dietsch, P. (2015). Rethinking sovereignty in international fiscal policy. *Review of International Studies, 37*(5), 2107.

Elkins, D. (2025). Rules, standards, and the value of certainty in tax law. *Berkeley Business Law Journal, 22*, 40.

IMF, & OECD. (2017). *Tax certainty* (Report for the G20 Finance Ministers). IMF/OECD. Retrieved August 10, 2025, from https://www.imf.org/external/np/g20/pdf/2017/031817.pdf

IMF, & OECD. (2018). *Update on tax certainty* (Report for the G20 Finance Ministers and Central Bank Governors). IMF/OECD. Retrieved August 10, 2025, from https://www.oecd.org/content/dam/oecd/en/topics/policy-issues/tax-administration/tax-certainty-update-oecd-imf-report-g20-finance-ministers-july-2018.pdf

[44] The B Team, 'A New Bar for Responsible Tax_ The B Team Responsible Tax Principles' (2018) <https://www.bteam.org/our-thinking/reports/responsibletax-2> accessed 10 August 2025.

[45] Ibid.

[46] The B Team (2024).

International Court of Justice (ICJ). (2025, July 23). *Obligations of States in respect of climate change (ICJ AO)*. Retrieved July 27, 2025, from https://www.icj-cij.org/sites/default/files/case-related/187/187-20250723-adv-01-00-en.pdf

Irish, C. R. (1986). Transfer pricing abuses and less developed countries. *University of Miami Inter-American Law Review, 18*, 91.

Oguttu, A. W. (2017). OECD multilateral instrument on treaty-related BEPS measures: Benefits, challenges and recommended options for South Africa and other developing countries. *South African Yearbook of International Law, 42*, 220.

Pagone, G. T. (2009). Tax uncertainty. *Melbourne University Law Review*. https://www5.austlii.edu.au/au/journals/MelbULawRw/2009/30.html

Reeves, L. (2022, September 1). Pillar One Amount A: Rules too complex, say corporations. *International Tax Review*.

Salacuse, J. (2021). *The law of investment treaties* (3rd ed.). Oxford University Press.

The B Team. (2024). *The B Team responsible tax principles: Accountability Report 2024*. Retrieved August 10, 2025, from https://www.bteam.org/our-thinking/reports/the-b-team-responsible-tax-principles-accountability-report-2024

Thuronyi, V., & Espejo, I. (2013). How can an excessive volume of tax disputes be dealt with? *IMF Legal Department*. Retrieved August 10, 2025, from https://www.imf.org/external/np/leg/tlaw/2013/eng/tdisputes.pdf

United Nations. (1992). *Rio Declaration on Environment and Development* (No. UN Doc A/CONF.151/26). UN Conference on Environment and Development.

United Nations. (2015). *Resolution 69/313: Addis Ababa Action Agenda of the Third International Conference on Financing for Development* (No. UN Doc A/RES/69/313). United Nations. https://www.un.org/esa/ffd/wp-content/uploads/2015/08/AAAA_Outcome.pdf

Inputs to the First Session: United Nations Ad Hoc Committee to Draft Terms of Reference for a United Nations Framework Convention on International Tax Cooperation. https://financing.desa.un.org/un-tax-convention/first-session

Inputs to the Second Session: United Nations Committee to Draft Terms of Reference for a United Nations Framework Convention on International Tax Cooperation. https://financing.desa.un.org/un-tax-convention/second-session

United Nations Department of Economic and Social Affairs (UNDESA). (2024, June 7). *Bureau's Proposal for the Zero Draft Terms of Reference for a United Nations Framework Convention on International Tax Cooperation*. Financing for Sustainable Development Office.

United Nations General Assembly (UNGA). (2023a). *Promotion of inclusive and effective international tax cooperation at the United Nations: Report of the Secretary-General 78/235 (SG Report)* (No. UN Doc A/78/235).

United Nations General Assembly (UNGA). (2023b). *Resolution 78/230: Promotion of Inclusive and Effective International Tax Cooperation at the United Nations* (No. UN Doc A/RES/78/230). United Nations General Assembly.

Vanderbruggen, E. (2001). State responsibility under customary international law in matters of taxation and tax competition. *Intertax, 29*(4), 115.

Vanderbruggen, E. (2025). Thoughts on the interpretation and desirability of tax carve-outs in investment treaties. *ICSID Review - Foreign Investment Law Journal, 40*(1), 114, 135.

Yusuf, B., Feriadi, & Indriawati, A. (2024). Tax disputes in the digital era: Challenges and opportunities toward legal certainty. *Jurnal Dedikasi Hukum, 4*(2), 2.

Chapter 6
Commitments for the Parties of the Framework Tax Convention

Abstract This chapter examines the six core commitments of the UN Framework Convention on International Tax Cooperation (FTC) as set out in UNGA 79/235, including fair allocation of taxing rights, combating tax evasion by high-net-worth individuals, and addressing illicit financial flows. It explores how these commitments aim to enhance sustainable development and equity, particularly for LMICs. The chapter also discusses the flexibility to add further commitments and the potential for protocols to operationalize these goals, addressing challenges like tax avoidance and dispute resolution to foster inclusive global tax governance.

Framework conventions typically articulate commitments or obligations in broad, rather than specific,[1] terms. Such conventions may stipulate that states adopt national policies to advance the convention's objectives,[2] publish or report on these policies,[3] provide education or capacity building,[4] or allocate funding.[5] The FTC delineates high-level commitments across six designated subjects. While obligations correspond to each commitment, their scope is likely to remain general, as outlined below.

---

[1] Bodansky (1999), p. 21.

[2] Vienna Convention for the Protection of the Ozone Layer (signed 22 March 1985, entered into force 22 September 1988) 1513 UNTS 293 art 2(1) and 2(2)(b); UNFCCC (n 39 in Chap. 2) art 4(2)(a).

[3] UNFCCC (n 39 in Chap. 2) art 4(1)(b).

[4] Convention on Biological Diversity (signed 5 June 1992, entered into force 29 December 1993) 1760 UNTS 79 (CBD) art 13.

[5] UNFCCC (n 39 in Chap. 2) art 4(3).

E. Vanderbruggen, *Reconstructing Global Tax Governance*, SpringerBriefs in Law, https://doi.org/10.1007/978-981-95-5617-5_6

6.1 'Fair Allocation of Taxing Rights, Including Equitable Taxation of Multinational Enterprises'

The reallocation of taxing rights to benefit LMICs constitutes a primary motivation for the majority of UN Members advocating for the FTC. Consequently, it is unsurprisingly identified as the foremost commitment within the FTC framework. Several approaches exist to formulate commitments concerning the allocation of taxing rights, particularly with respect to multinational enterprises (MNEs) and the digital economy.

For instance, transfer pricing by MNEs may form the basis of a commitment, with a particular emphasis on CbC reporting, as highlighted by several states during the Ad Hoc Committee's discussions.[6] Another example includes commitments by certain states to support LMICs in enhancing their transfer pricing tax audit capabilities and providing access to relevant transfer-pricing-related data and information.

6.2 'Addressing Tax Evasion and Avoidance by High-Net-Worth Individuals'

The taxation of high-net-worth individuals has emerged as a significant issue within the FTC,[7] intersecting with themes such as equity, tax avoidance and evasion, IFFs, and DRM.

At the Ad Hoc Committee, both HICs and LMICs, including Algeria, Brazil, and Norway,[8] underscored the challenges of taxing high-net-worth individuals, typically residents of the state seeking to impose such taxes. This issue, traditionally situated within the sovereign power to tax, poses particular difficulties for LMICs in accessing financial and tax information held overseas, where such individuals often conceal their wealth.[9] Consequently, the FTC incorporates one or more high-level obligations to address this challenge. Kenya proposed designating the taxation of high-net-worth individuals as the subject of an initial protocol, arguing that effective action requires international tax cooperation. Kenya further noted that existing mechanisms for information exchange are inadequate.[10]

---

[6] Brazil, 3rd meeting of the First Session (29 April 2024) (n 44 in Chap. 2); Norway and Sweden, 2nd Meeting of the First Session (26 April 2024) (n 44 in Chap. 2); India, 2nd Meeting of the First Session (26 April 2024) (n 44 in Chap. 2).

[7] It was not specifically mentioned in the Addis Agenda (United Nations, 2015) or the SG Report [United Nations General Assembly (UNGA), 2023a].

[8] Kenya, 4th meeting of the First Session (29 April 2024) (n 44 in Chap. 2): 'High network individuals stash their assets in foreign jurisdictions and the country where those assets were sourced from would lack the required information or reach to be able to tax those assets effectively […] but sheltering the worth in other jurisdictions'.

[9] Ibid.

[10] Kenya, 4th meeting of the First Session (29 April 2024) (n 44 in Chap. 2): 'But in our experience, we have found that it is not fully effective because the requested jurisdictions can find ways to not exchange that information'.

Several HICs view the taxation of high-net-worth individuals in LMICs as a critical component of enhancing DRM.[11] This perspective could be leveraged in future negotiations to advance DRM objectives.

Commissioned by the Brazilian G20 Presidency, Professor Gabriel Zucman proposed a 2% annual baseline tax on the wealth of the world's billionaires.[12] Wealth taxes were recognised as a potential means to bolster DRM through high-net-worth individuals, though opinions at the Ad Hoc Committee diverged on their efficacy. The Bahamas cautioned that 'the risk of capital flight due to a wealth tax could be devastating to small, vulnerable developing countries'.[13]

Notably, HICs and LMICs appear more aligned on the issue of taxing high-net-worth individuals than on other aspects of the FTC, though views differ on its integration into the framework. Several HICs supported the inclusion of a commitment on this matter,[14] while others opposed it, arguing that such taxation should remain a matter of domestic sovereignty.[15] Ultimately, the taxation of high-net-worth individuals was incorporated as both a commitment and a candidate for an early protocol.

Another dimension of cooperation under this commitment involves capacity building for DRM through progressive taxation[16] or wealth taxes, which could contribute to reducing inequality and eradicating poverty.[17]

6.3 'The Achievement of Sustainable Development in its Three Dimensions, Economic, Social and Environmental'

The TOR of the FTC incorporate a high-level commitment linking international tax cooperation to economic, social, and environmental dimensions of sustainable development.

The centrality of sustainable development as a global community objective, particularly in financing contexts such as the Addis Ababa Action Agenda, significantly influences the FTC.[18] Consequently, the UN has embedded a high-level commitment in the TOR explicitly referencing sustainable development.

[11] The Netherlands, Inputs to the First Session (n 44 in Chap. 2): 'The Netherlands takes the view that taxing high-net-worth individuals is one of many factors in improving DRM. Other factors include digitization of tax administration, environmental and carbon taxes and strategies for realizing effective taxation of high net worth'.

[12] Zucman (2024).

[13] The Bahamas, 5th Meeting of the Second Session (31 July 2024) (n 44 in Chap. 2): 'The risk of capital flight because of a wealth tax could be devastating to small, vulnerable developing countries'.

[14] Belgium, 4th Meeting of the First Session (29 April 2024) (n 44 in Chap. 2).

[15] United States, 4th Meeting of the First Session (29 April 2024) (n 44 in Chap. 2).

[16] United Nations (2015), para 22.

[17] Japan, 6th Meeting of the First Session (30 April 2024) (n 44 in Chap. 2).

[18] United Nations (2015), para 1.

This commitment yields several implications. Broadly, it supports future rule-making under the FTC, ensuring that tax cooperation initiatives contribute to all facets of sustainable development. Sustainable development may serve as a benchmark, akin to established principles such as 'good faith' or 'legitimate expectations', guiding the creation, evaluation, or interpretation of future cooperation mechanisms within the FTC. This commitment may also inform the development of more detailed obligations at a later stage. Moreover, a high-level commitment to advancing sustainable development could influence the design of taxing rights in the digital economy. For instance, proponents of this perspective may take the view that an FTC MS endorsing this commitment might find it challenging to justify maintaining a taxing rights structure that deprives LMICs of tax revenue from the online economy.

It is pertinent to consider the intended beneficiaries of sustainable development within the context of the FTC. Rather than an abstract or global conception of sustainable development, the reference should be interpreted as applying specifically to individual states or groups of states. This implies that the FTC should evaluate the outcomes of the international tax system, particularly as every state requires fiscal revenue to fund its sustainable development objectives. The allocation of taxing rights, which directly influences revenue generation, is closely related to this issue. The suggestion is that taxing rights structures that result in negligible revenue for certain states may contravene the commitment to tax cooperation that supports sustainable development.[19]

The high-level commitment to sustainable development may obligate FTC Members to adopt processes that actively promote sustainable development.[20] Nevertheless, it may be challenging to assess which tax measures are inconsistent with a commitment to foster sustainable development. For instance, consider international cooperation aimed at eliminating tax incentives. On the one hand, certain tax incentives may harm the efficiency of the international tax system. On the other hand, tax incentives may be justifiable to promote economic growth -a necessary element of sustainable development- and just transition.

In practical terms, this commitment provides overarching support for tax cooperation initiatives that align with economic, social, and environmental objectives. Among the proposals discussed at the Ad Hoc Committee, cooperation on environmental taxes emerged as particularly prominent. Carbon and other environmental taxes were frequently highlighted,[21] with Germany noting their potential to enhance DRM and finance SDGs.[22] Similarly, a protocol to coordinate the phasing out of domestic tax incentives linked to environmentally harmful activities was identified as a potential area for future cooperation.

---

[19] See below Sect. 7.3.

[20] Boyle et al. (2021), p. 127.

[21] The Bahamas, 6th Meeting of the First Session (30 April 2024) (n 44 in Chap. 2): 'We call for the recognition of environmental taxes, sometimes referred to as a carbon tax'. See also, Comments by Sri Lanka in the same meeting.

[22] Germany, 4th Meeting of the First Session (29 April 2024) (n 44 in Chap. 2).

6.4 'Effective Mutual Administrative Assistance in Tax Matters'

A pivotal instrument for enhancing international cooperation in tax enforcement is the Convention on Mutual Administrative Assistance in Tax Matters (MAAC),[23] which facilitates the establishment of bilateral Tax Information Exchange Agreements (TIEAs). Jointly developed by the OECD and the Council of Europe in 1988, the Convention emerged in response to the OECD's identification of transparency deficits as a key issue in tax competition.[24] Subsequently, in 2002, the OECD released a Model TIEA, formulated by the Working Group on Effective Exchange of Information, established under the auspices of the Global Forum.

Founded in 2000 by the OECD, the Global Forum aims to expedite information exchange between Members and offshore financial centres. Following the 2008 financial crisis, G20 Leaders, at the London Summit in April 2009, proclaimed that "the era of banking secrecy is over," signalling a robust commitment to reform and laying the groundwork for subsequent initiatives.[25] Comprising 172 members, including predominantly LMICs and all G20 nations, the Global Forum combats offshore tax evasion by promoting international standards on transparency and information exchange for tax purposes, monitoring and reviewing their implementation, and providing capacity-building and technical assistance to LMICs.

The Global Forum promotes international standards encompassing Exchange of Information on Request (EOIR) and Automatic Exchange of Information (AEOI). The former facilitates targeted requests for information to tax authorities for the purposes of tax investigations, while the latter enables the automatic exchange of a predefined dataset between tax authorities, with a particular emphasis on transactions involving crypto-assets through the Crypto-Asset Reporting Framework (CARF).

State practice in response to calls for reduced constraints on tax information exchange has been substantial. In 2009, 74 of the 143 jurisdictions reviewed imposed restrictions on accessing and sharing banking information; today, only a small number of jurisdictions retain such impediments. In total, 68 jurisdictions have amended their national legislation to facilitate access to banking information for tax information exchange purposes. Furthermore, numerous states have abolished bearer shares, a mechanism frequently used to conceal the beneficial ownership of companies.[26]

Despite the establishment of the Africa Initiative by the Global Forum in 2014[27] to enhance African engagement, participation by African countries in tax information exchange remains challenging, primarily due to financial and capacity

---

[23] OECD (2025a).

[24] OECD (1998).

[25] Group of Twenty (G20) (2009).

[26] OECD (2025b), p. 11.

[27] OECD (n.d.).

constraints.[28] For instance, while the United Kingdom issued 1856 EOIR requests in 2016 alone, the combined total from Africa Initiative members—comprising Cameroon, Burkina Faso, Ghana, Kenya, Liberia, Morocco, Nigeria, and Uganda—amounted to only 79 requests over the first 3 years of the initiative (2015–2017). Nevertheless, the implementation of EOIR has yielded notable tax revenue gains in several African jurisdictions. Uganda, for example, recovered over $9 million in taxes during the 2015–2016 period, while Burkina Faso secured an estimated $2.4 million from its initial requests.[29] Similarly, South Africa collected $62.24 million through a settlement with a single taxpayer in 2013.[30] Given the potential benefits of enhanced tax transparency, administration, and compliance for African nations, a more robust role for the African Union is essential in prioritising information sharing within African countries and securing tax information exchange agreements with other jurisdictions, alongside increased support from G20 leaders.

The SG Report identified significant challenges with the Global Forum,[31] prompting the Ad Hoc Committee to incorporate international exchange of information within the FTC and designate two non-priority protocols to address this issue.

HICs, notably the United States, highlighted the Global Forum's substantial progress in facilitating international information exchange, arguing that it would be redundant for the UN to pursue similar efforts.[32] This perspective sparked a robust debate at the Ad Hoc Committee. Several LMICs contended that the Global Forum's framework is not universally effective, while many HICs challenged this assertion.[33] Ghana argued that merely counting the number of LMICs participating in the Global Forum was inadequate; the focus should instead be on how many can effectively implement its system, which was established before most LMICs joined. Ghana suggested that successful implementation rates among LMICs remain low.[34]

Kenya, Nigeria, and Senegal advocated for designating information exchange as a priority protocol, but this proposal was not incorporated into the TOR. Instead,

---

[28] Monkam et al. (2018).

[29] Ibid 5.

[30] Ibid 5.

[31] United Nations General Assembly (UNGA) (2023a), paras 39–44.

[32] United States, 11th Meeting of the First Session (3 May 2024) (n 44 in Chap. 2): 'We appreciate the points made by the distinguished delegates that some countries do not yet receive the full benefits of the exchange of information. However, we believe that this can be addressed and is currently being addressed through the capacity building efforts undertaken by the Global Forum [...]. Out of the 193 member states at the UN, 171 are members of the Global Forum. The majority of the members of the Global Forum are developing countries, and the Global Forum has expended substantial resources over the last 20 years to assist jurisdictions and implementing the standards on transparency and exchange of information. We do not see the benefit of the UN taking on the same or similar work or creating different standards that would risk fracturing the current international norms'.

[33] Canada, 12th Meeting of the First Session (3 May 2024) (n 44 in Chap. 2).

[34] Ghana, 11th Meeting of the First Session (3 May 2024) (n 44 in Chap. 2).

alongside mutual administrative assistance, it was included as a non-priority protocol.[35]

6.5 'Addressing Tax-Related Illicit Financial Flows, Tax Avoidance, Tax Evasion and Harmful Tax Practices'

This high-level commitment encompasses issues unlikely to face significant opposition, with IFFs identified as a potential subject for an early protocol, ranking prominently among the priorities of the FTC. The Addis Ababa Action Agenda reinforces the focus on IFFs in the context of tax evasion.[36] The SG Report underscores the role of the FTC in curbing tax-related IFFs, stating: 'Some challenges, such as eliminating IFFs, necessitate global action, as a few jurisdictions can undermine the efforts of the majority'.[37] The SG Report expresses confidence in the consensus on strengthening international tax cooperation to combat tax avoidance, evasion, and IFFs, which disproportionately deplete resources from LMICs.[38] It further suggests that 'if sufficient agreement exists on certain action items, some protocols could be negotiated concurrently with the framework convention, including, for instance, a protocol addressing illicit financial flows'.[39] Several LMICs endorsed the development of an early protocol on IFFs.[40]

The reference to tax evasion is expected, as it is often synonymous with 'illicit' in the taxation context, and its linkage with DRM was noted by several states.[41]

The inclusion of 'tax avoidance' is less straightforward, as it is not inherently illicit. However, at the Ad Hoc Committee, 'tax avoidance and evasion' were often treated as a composite term, appearing analogous in discussions.[42] Neither the African Group's submissions nor the Zero Draft TOR explicitly referenced 'avoidance',[43] though the SG Report highlighted 'aggressive tax avoidance'[44] and 'tax avoidance'.[45]

---

[35] Kenya, Nigeria and Senegal, First Session, 13th Meeting of the First Session (6 May 2024) (n 44 in Chap. 2).

[36] United Nations (2015), para 23.

[37] United Nations General Assembly (UNGA) (2023a), para 58.

[38] Ibid, para 71.

[39] Ibid, para 56.

[40] For example, Algeria and Brazil, 1st Meeting of the First Session (26 April 2024) (n 44 in Chap. 2).

[41] For example, India, 4th Meeting of the First Session (29 April 2024) (n 44 in Chap. 2).

[42] For example, Sri Lanka, Austria and Canada, 14th Meeting of the First Session (6 May 2024) (n 44 in Chap. 2).

[43] Nigeria on behalf of the African Group, Inputs to the First Session (n 44 in Chap. 2).

[44] United Nations General Assembly (UNGA) (2023a), para 5.

[45] Ibid, para 71.

The high-level commitment to addressing IFFs, tax evasion, and avoidance within the FTC has multiple implications. Primarily, it establishes a general obligation for Members to take action in these areas. This commitment could manifest in measures such as enacting national policies to enhance financial information collection, improve transparency, and reduce financial secrecy, potentially through enhanced IFF monitoring and reporting within the FTC or its protocols.[46]

The commitment also addresses 'harmful tax practices'. Opting for this term over 'harmful tax competition' allows for a balanced approach, addressing both excessive tax competition and the need to moderate measures that counteract other states' tax exemptions. This aligns with Action 5 of the OECD/G20 BEPS initiative: 'Counter harmful tax practices more effectively, taking into account transparency and substance'.[47] The Secretary-General noted concerns that the implementation of Pillar Two by some countries could infringe on tax sovereignty and hinder investment incentives through tax credits.[48] The African Group proposed at the First Session that 'harmful tax regimes' be included among commitments and early protocols.[49] The Zero Draft TOR, however, incorporated 'harmful tax practices' as a proposed commitment.[50]

Consequently, the FTC may establish high-level obligations to phase out excessive tax incentives that erode the tax bases of other states. Simultaneously, it may recognise that states should refrain from enacting policies that neutralise reasonable investment or environmental tax incentives of other states, except under specific circumstances.

6.6 'Effective Prevention and Resolution of Tax Disputes'

The prospect of the FTC introducing innovative mechanisms for resolving tax disputes is compelling. The SG Report opened avenues for addressing disputes both between states and between states and taxpayers, noting that while some domestic legal systems may provide objective forums for dispute resolution, not all are adequate. Consequently, a fully inclusive and effective international tax cooperation system necessitates robust, principled, and effective processes for preventing and

[46] Austria, 4th Meeting of the First Session (29 April 2024) (n 44 in Chap. 2): 'Helping countries, each other in better understanding where the tax money is flowing'.

[47] Group of Twenty (G20) (2013).

[48] United Nations General Assembly (UNGA) (2023a), para 38. See also, Ghana, 11th Meeting of the First Session (3 May 2024) (n 44 in Chap. 2): 'Where a particular region of the world decides to come up with practices that puts another region of the world at a disadvantage. It is a harmful tax practice'.

[49] Nigeria on behalf of the African Group, Inputs to the First Session (n 44 in Chap. 2) items 6–7.

[50] See the United Nations Department of Economic and Social Affairs (UNDESA) (2024). This is similar to the Addis Agenda (United Nations, 2015), para 27.

resolving tax disputes, aligned with domestic law and international commitments when domestic mechanisms prove insufficient.[51]

Resolution 78/230 explicitly mandated the inclusion of dispute settlement provisions within the FTC,[52] a directive already reflected in the Zero Draft TOR.[53] However, the African Group's Written Input prior to the First Session did not address this issue.

Discussions at the Ad Hoc Committee reveal a lack of consensus on a unified approach to tax dispute settlement. For instance, Brazil and Jamaica highlighted benefits for taxpayers,[54] whereas the Bahamas focused on intergovernmental tax disputes.[55] During the First Session, the Chair underscored dispute settlement as a critical functional component of the FTC, referencing Resolution 78/230 and citing LMICs' negative experiences with dispute settlement in trade and investment contexts, particularly due to funding and capacity constraints.[56]

At the 2025 organisational session, tax dispute settlement was designated as the subject of the second early protocol.[57] The FTC might adopt a non-binding dispute resolution mechanism, similar to that of the United Nations Framework Convention on Climate Change (UNFCCC), potentially combining consultations with (occasionally mandatory) conciliation through a body of experts or a commission with equal representation from each party, empowered to issue advisory awards. Such an approach may be palatable to many states.[58] Resolution 78/230 sets a more ambitious goal, advocating for new commitments to address tax-related investment disputes, including through financial assistance and capacity building.[59]

Establishing a mandatory and binding system for tax dispute resolution within the FTC is challenging. The OECD's Multilateral Convention to Implement Tax Treaty Related Measures to Prevent BEPS (MLI) sought to introduce mandatory binding arbitration to amend bilateral tax treaties, with limited success.[60] While

[51] United Nations General Assembly (UNGA) (2023a), para 18.

[52] United Nations General Assembly (UNGA) (2023b).

[53] United Nations Department of Economic and Social Affairs (UNDESA) (2024), para 13: 'The framework convention should also include the following additional substantive and procedural elements: [...] dispute settlement mechanism.' The final outcome has maintained this language: United Nations General Assembly (UNGA) (2024), para 13.

[54] Brazil, 5th Meeting of the Second Session (31 July 2024) (n 44 in Chap. 2); Jamaica, 7th Meeting of the Second Session (1 August 2024) (n 44 in Chap. 2).

[55] The Bahamas, 6th Meeting of the First Session (30 April 2024) (n 44 in Chap. 2), referring to 'unilateral blacklisting of jurisdictions' by the European Union; Oei (2022), p. 219. The Council of the European Union did this for the first time on 5 December 2017: Council of the European Union (2017). Presently, the 'EU List of Non-Cooperative Jurisdictions for Tax Purposes' can be found here: <https://www.consilium.europa.eu/en/policies/eu-list-of-non-cooperative-jurisdictions/>.

[56] Chair presentation, 10th Meeting of the First Session (2 May 2024) (n 44 in Chap. 2).

[57] United Nations (2025).

[58] UNFCCC (n 39 in Chap. 2) art 14. See also, Bodansky (1999), pp. 27–28.

[59] UNCTAD (2022).

[60] OECD (2017), art 19; Noonan and Plekhanova (2023), p. 437.

LMICs generally oppose such measures, it is noteworthy that certain states, which do not currently employ mandatory arbitration, indicated at the Ad Hoc Committee a potential openness to exploring this option.[61]

6.7 The Protocols

The United Nations will concurrently commence drafting the FTC and at least two protocols addressing specific issues with binding obligations.[62] These protocols constitute distinct, legally binding instruments under the FTC. Accession to the FTC does not automatically entail participation in its protocols, allowing states to join a protocol either upon becoming a party to the FTC or at a later stage.

The Ad Hoc Committee dedicated substantial effort to reaching a compromise on the selection of subject matters for the early protocols. The African Group advocated for prioritising 'tax-related illicit financial flows', 'taxation of the digital economy', and cross-border services as early protocols,[63] notably asserting that a protocol on the digital economy would represent 'a quick win for all involved'.[64]

While UN Members have agreed in the TOR that the first protocol will address taxation of income derived from provision of cross-border services in an increasingly digitalized and globalized economy,[65] the subject of the second protocol had to be decided based on a list of priority areas set out in the TOR, including: taxation of the digitalized economy; measures against tax-related illicit financial flows; prevention and resolution of tax disputes; and addressing tax evasion and avoidance by high-net worth individuals and ensuring their effective taxation in relevant Members.[66] The selection of the topic of the second protocol was an important task of the FTC organizational session between 3 to 6 February 2025, resulting in 'prevention and resolution of tax disputes' being selected.[67]

6.8 Capacity Building

Capacity building is often regarded as a panacea for addressing deficiencies in tax policy and administration. The SG Report acknowledges the existence of substantial capacity-building initiatives but highlighted that the technical assistance

[61] Korea, 6th Meeting of the First Session (30 April 2024) (n 44 in Chap. 2).

[62] United Nations General Assembly (UNGA) (2023b), point 6(e).

[63] As suggested by the African Group in their Written Inputs to the Second Session (n 44 in Chap. 2), para 14.

[64] Ibid, para 15.

[65] United Nations General Assembly (UNGA) (2024), para 15.

[66] Ibid, para 16.

[67] International Institute for Sustainable Development (IISD) (n.d.).

provided frequently fails to align with the needs or immediate priorities of LMICs.[68] In many instances, the Secretary-General notes, HICs prioritise the type of capacity support they wish to offer, rather than responding to the specific requirements articulated by LMICs.[69] Consequently, resources are often expended on efforts that yield inadequate practical outcomes. Following the SG Report, Resolution 78/230 linked capacity building to the ability of states to participate fully in the decision-making processes of the international tax system, reflecting the Secretary-General's observations.[70]

Drawing from the SG Report and discussions at the Ad Hoc Committee, two distinct forms of capacity building emerge. The first pertains to strengthening the national tax systems of LMICs, which is closely tied to international tax guidance.[71] This objective enjoys broad consensus among HICs[72] and LMICs and was included in the African Group's Written Input prior to the First Session, particularly in the context of tax dispute settlement.[73] The FTC could offer a novel platform for cooperation in this area.[74] Currently, coordination among donors of capacity-building activities is informal and fragmented, lacking formal international mechanisms that afford LMICs equal decision-making authority. Drawing parallels with the UNFCCC, where capacity building falls under the purview of the Subsidiary Body for Scientific and Technological Advice, which advises the Conference of the Parties on scientific and technological matters, a similar structure could be envisioned for

---

[68] United Nations General Assembly (UNGA) (2023a), para 69.

[69] Ibid: 'Current capacity-building activities by international organizations, regional tax organizations, government development agencies, civil society organizations and academia are often focused on assisting developing countries in implementing existing tax rules and improving tax administration related to those tax rules. However, as indicated by developing countries during the special meeting of the Economic and Social Council on international cooperation in tax matters in 2023, if those rules do not respond adequately to their circumstances, technical assistance to implement those rules would not address their most immediate concerns and needs for capacity building in tax policy and administration'. See United Nations Economic and Social Council (ECOSOC) (2023), para 14.

[70] United Nations General Assembly (UNGA) (2023b), p. 2: '*Recognizing further* that inclusiveness in international tax cooperation involves capacity-building and support to developing countries so that they can effectively participate in the full range of international tax cooperation in an equitable manner, while stressing that capacity-building efforts should fully take into account the needs and priorities of developing countries'.

[71] This includes the complex guidance issued under the OECD/G20 Base Erosion and Profit Shifting Project, 'Statement on a Two-Pillar Solution to Address the Tax Challenges Arising from the Digitalisation of the Economy' (OECD/G20, 2021), and OECD, *OECD Transfer Pricing Guidelines for Multinational Enterprises and Tax Administrations 2022* (OECD Publishing 2022) (OECD 2022).

[72] See, for example, the Written Inputs before the First Session by the United States and Germany (n 44 in Chap. 2), both connecting capacity building with DRM.

[73] Written Inputs by the African Group before the First Session (n 44 in Chap. 2) on settlement of tax disputes, as a commitment in relation to 'technical cooperation with respect to exchange of expertise and best practices': at item 6(x).

[74] As the African Group suggested in their Written Inputs to the Second Session (n 44 in Chap. 2), para 11: 'We propose that the convention should seek to or coordinate all capacity building efforts of the United Nations. This will ensure the effectiveness and inclusiveness of such an effort'.

the FTC.[75] Such a framework could facilitate more effective cooperation in capacity building to enhance DRM, increase the transparency of international efforts, and amplify the voice of LMICs in identifying their specific needs. It would also enable the evaluation of the effectiveness of such initiatives.

The second form of capacity building focuses on enabling LMICs to participate more meaningfully in international tax cooperation. As the SG Report noted: 'As a practical matter, it can be challenging for a country with limited international tax expertise to influence decision-making processes in these forums'.[76] While some funding is available through mechanisms like the OECD/G20 IF or the Global Forum, it often fails to cover all associated costs or is not provided in a timely manner to keep pace with rapid developments in international tax policy.[77]

6.9 Governance

The decision in favour of the basic governance structure of a framework convention was affirmed by the General Assembly in Resolution 78/230, prior to the commencement of the Ad Hoc Committee's work.

The TOR stipulates that the FTC will establish an organisational structure modelled on the UNFCCC. This envisages a 'Conference of the Parties' (COP) as the supreme body, with representation from all parties. Collectively, these parties would make decisions for the FTC, though it remains uncertain whether such decisions will require a simple majority, a qualified majority, or consensus. The Secretariat, as envisioned by many UN Members, would comprise a team equipped with sufficient resources and technical expertise to organise COP meetings, compile information on commitments, facilitate consensus and protocol development, and execute other responsibilities under the FTC.

A proposal by Japan to include provisions for reservations to the FTC was not incorporated into the TOR, though this omission is not necessarily conclusive.[78]

6.10 Relationship with OECD Work

The SG Report and Resolution 78/230 recommended that the FTC should not seek to supplant existing OECD initiatives but rather 'leverage existing strengths and address gaps'[79] while identifying 'complementarities'.[80] This approach was

[75] UNFCCC (n 39 in Chap. 2) art 9.

[76] United Nations General Assembly (UNGA) (2023a), para 44.

[77] Christensen et al. (2020).

[78] Japan, Inputs to the First Session (n 44 in Chap. 2).

[79] United Nations General Assembly (UNGA) (2023a), para 49.

[80] United Nations General Assembly (UNGA) (2023b), point 6(d).

enthusiastically endorsed by HICs. Article 6 of Resolution 78/230 incorporates this directive alongside other mandates, such as 'taking into account the needs, priorities, and capacities of all countries' (subsequently enshrined as a principle in the TOR), adopting a 'sustainable development perspective' (reflected as both a principle and a commitment in the TOR), and considering 'the need for flexibility and resilience' (also adopted as a principle in the TOR). However, the call to consider complementarities with OECD work was not elevated to a principle. Instead, it was included in the Zero Draft TOR and the final TOR but 'relegated'[81] to Part IV, 'Approaches and Time Frame for Negotiation'.[82] The African Group proposed omitting references to 'complementarity' entirely, expressing concern that 'such elements would permanently consign the Convention to a secondary role, merely filling gaps left by other fora'.[83]

OECD members and the EU expressed disappointment that the TOR does not include a principle explicitly referencing OECD initiatives.[84] The EU advocated for a framework that avoids duplicating OECD efforts but complements existing initiatives to ensure a coherent approach to global tax cooperation, stating: 'Consistency with ongoing work and consensus achieved in other international fora should be a guiding principle for any tax-related international cooperation undertaken at the UN'.[85] Several countries echoed this sentiment, cautioning against 'duplication'.[86]

References

Bodansky, D. (1999). *The Framework Convention/Protocol Approach* (No. Paper 1; Technical Briefing Series). World Health Organization (WHO). https://iris.who.int/handle/10665/65355

Boyle, A. E., Redgwell, C., & Birnie, P. W. (2021). *International law and the environment* (4th ed.). Oxford University Press.

Christensen, R. C., Hearson, M., & Randriamanalina, T. (2020). *At the table, off the menu: Assessing the participation of lower-income countries in global tax negotiations* (No. Working Paper 115). International Centre of Tax and Development, Institute of Development Studies. https://www.ictd.ac/publication/table-off-menu-participation-lower-income-countries-tax-negotiations

Council of the European Union. (2017). *Council conclusions on the EU list of non-cooperative jurisdictions for tax purposes* (No. 15429/17). https://www.consilium.europa.eu/en/policies/eu-list-of-non-cooperative-jurisdictions/

[81] United States, Inputs to the Second Session (n 44 in Chap. 2).

[82] United Nations General Assembly (UNGA) (2024), para 22.

[83] African Group, Inputs to the Second Session (n 44 in Chap. 2).

[84] See the statement by the European Union dated 29 July 2024 (European Union, Inputs to the Second Session (n 44 in Chap. 2) proposing that commitments should be on a complementary basis. Conversely, United Nations General Assembly (UNGA) (2024), para 6 does state that the FTC should reflect resolutions 77/244 and 78/230.

[85] 1st Meeting of the First Session (26 April 2024) (n 44 in Chap. 2).

[86] For example, the European Union, Belgium, The Philippines and Singapore, 1st Meeting of the First Session (26 April 2024) (n 44 in Chap. 2).

Group of Twenty (G20). (2009). *G20 leaders' statement at the London summit*. Retrieved August 10, 2025, from https://g7g20-documents.org/database/document/2009-g20-united-kingdom-leaders-leaders-language-london-summit-leaders-statement

Group of Twenty (G20). (2013). *Tax annex to the Saint Petersburg G20 leaders declaration*. Retrieved March 11, 2025, from https://www.g20germany.de/Content/DE/_Anlagen/G7_G20/G20-erklaerung-petersburg-annex-en___blob=publicationFile&v=1.pdf

International Institute for Sustainable Development (IISD). (n.d.). *Summary report, 3–6 February 2025: Organizational session for the intergovernmental negotiations for the UN Framework Convention on International Tax Cooperation*. Retrieved October 8, 2025, from https://enb.iisd.org/un-framework-convention-international-tax-cooperation-organizational-session-summary

Monkam, N., Ibrahim, G., Davis, W., & von Haldenwang, C. (2018). *Tax transparency and exchange of information (EOI): Priorities for Africa*. T20 Argentina Policy Brief. Retrieved August 10, 2025, from https://t20argentina.org/wp-content/uploads/2018/07/TF5-5.2-Taxation.pdf

Noonan, C., & Plekhanova, V. (2023). Mandatory binding dispute resolution in the base erosion and profit shifting (BEPS) two pillar solution. *International and Comparative Law Quarterly, 72*, 437.

OECD. (1998). *Harmful tax competition: An emerging global issue*.

OECD. (2017). *Multilateral convention to implement tax treaty related measures to prevent base erosion and profit shifting* (No. OECD/LEGAL/0432; p. Article 19). https://www.oecd.org/tax/treaties/multilateral-convention-to-implement-tax-treaty-related-measures-to-prevent-BEPS.htm

OECD. (2022). *Transfer pricing guidelines for multinational enterprises and tax administrations 2022*. Organisation for Economic Cooperation and Development.

OECD. (2025a). *Jurisdictions participating in the Convention on Mutual Administrative Assistance in Tax Matters*. Retrieved August 10, 2025, from https://www.oecd.org/content/dam/oecd/en/topics/policy-sub-issues/convention-on-mutual-administrative-assistance-in-tax-matters/status_of_convention.pdf/_jcr_content/renditions/original./status_of_convention.pdf

OECD. (2025b). *Taking stock of progress on transparency and exchange of information for tax purposes: OECD and Global Forum Report to G20 Finance Ministers and Central Bank Governors* (p. 11). Retrieved August 10, 2025, from https://www.oecd.org/en/publications/2025/07/taking-stock-of-progress-on-transparency-and-exchange-of-information-for-tax-purposes_cf7047a4.html

OECD. (n.d.). *Global forum on transparency and exchange of information for tax purposes*. Retrieved October 8, 2025, from https://www.oecd.org/en/networks/global-forum-tax-transparency/what-we-do/africa-initiative.html

OECD/G20. (2021). *Statement on a two-pillar solution to address the tax challenges arising from the digitalisation of the economy*.

Oei, S.-Y. (2022). World tax policy in the world tax polity? An event history analysis of OECD/G20 BEPS Inclusive Framework Membership. *Yale Journal of International Law, 47*(Summer), 199.

UNCTAD. (2022). *Facts on Investor–State Arbitrations in 2021: With a special focus on tax-related ISDS cases* (p. 5). IAA Issues Note. Retrieved March 11, 2025, from https://investmentpolicy.unctad.org/

United Nations. (2015). *Resolution 69/313: Addis Ababa action agenda of the third international conference on financing for development* (No. UN Doc A/RES/69/313). United Nations. https://www.un.org/esa/ffd/wp-content/uploads/2015/08/AAAA_Outcome.pdf

Inputs to the First Session: United Nations Ad Hoc Committee to Draft Terms of Reference for a United Nations Framework Convention on International Tax Cooperation. https://financing.desa.un.org/un-tax-convention/first-session

Inputs to the Second Session: United Nations Committee to Draft Terms of Reference for a United Nations Framework Convention on International Tax Cooperation. https://financing.desa.un.org/un-tax-convention/second-session

United Nations. (2025). *Subject of Protocol II: Draft decision by the Chair* (No. UN Doc A/AC.298/CRP.5). Intergovernmental Negotiating Committee on the United Nations Framework Convention on International Tax Cooperation.

United Nations Department of Economic and Social Affairs (UNDESA). (2024, June 7). *Bureau's proposal for the zero draft terms of reference for a United Nations Framework Convention on International Tax Cooperation*. Financing for Sustainable Development Office.

United Nations Economic and Social Council (ECOSOC). (2023). *Official summary of the special meeting on international cooperation in tax matters* (para 14).

United Nations General Assembly (UNGA). (2023a). *Promotion of inclusive and effective International Tax Cooperation at the United Nations: Report of the Secretary-General 78/235 (SG Report)* (No. UN Doc A/78/235).

United Nations General Assembly (UNGA). (2023b). *Resolution 78/230: Promotion of inclusive and effective International Tax Cooperation at the United Nations* (No. UN Doc A/RES/78/230). United Nations General Assembly.

United Nations General Assembly (UNGA). (2024). *Chair's proposal for draft terms of reference (TOR)* (No. UN Doc A/AC.295/2024/L.4.).

Zucman, G. (2024). A blueprint for a coordinated minimum effective taxation standard for ultra-high-net-worth individuals. *EU Tax Observatory*. Retrieved March 11, 2025, from https://www.taxobservatory.eu/publication/a-blueprint-for-a-coordinated-minimum-effective-taxation-standard-for-ultra-high-net-worth-individuals/

Chapter 7
Sustainable Development, Fairness, and Human Rights as Proposed Foundational Principles for the International Tax System

Abstract This is chapter analyses the FTC's turn towards foundational principles reflecting community interests for the international tax system. The chapter focuses on three core principles that the FTC proposes to incorporate into international tax cooperation, notably sustainable development, fairness or equity, and respect for human rights obligations. The chapter contextualizes each of these core principles and its current interactions with international taxation. It explores how sustainable development, alongside equity and human rights, seeks to align tax systems with global goals like the SDGs. The chapter assesses the principle's normative potential through systemic integration under VCLT Article 31(3)(c), its challenges in reshaping utilitarian DTA provisions, and its role in ensuring fiscal adequacy for climate and human rights objectives.

7.1 Turning to Core Principles

Arguably, among the most novel aspects of the FTC is its invocation of several foundational legal principles that are proposed for the international tax system the FTC seeks to establish. As was highlighted in the discussion above, reflections of these principles are found throughout FTCs objectives and principles, as well as some of its commitments. These include the principle of sustainable development, equity (or fairness, reflected in participatory inclusion and fair taxing rights), human rights as well other principles that will not be examined in detail in what follows, such as legal certainty, transparency, and sovereignty.[1]

To contextualize the FTC's shift towards foundational principles, it is instructive to revisit Simma's definition of (universal) community interests as 'a consensus according to which respect for certain fundamental values is not to be left to the free disposition of States individually or inter se but is recognised and sanctioned

[1] United Nations General Assembly (UNGA) (2024), art 9.

E. Vanderbruggen, *Reconstructing Global Tax Governance*, SpringerBriefs in Law, https://doi.org/10.1007/978-981-95-5617-5_7

by international law as a matter of concern to all States'.[2] Simma identified these interests as encompassing international peace and security, environmental protection, human rights, the common heritage of mankind, and solidarity between HICs and LMICs.[3] This perspective views international law as more than a collection of transactional bilateral agreements, adopting a human-centric approach that prioritises the interests of the global community, including all human beings. As Simma notes: 'a rising awareness of the common interests of the international community […] has begun to change the nature of international law profoundly'.[4]

More broadly, community interests have been defined to include non-universal values and interests shared across borders, transcending the reciprocal exchanges of benefits between states.[5] For example, arguments have been made that certain aspects of international investment treaties and world trade law respond to community interests, by supporting legal certainty and predictability, and economic growth.[6]

Given the bilateralist origins of much of the treaty rules governing the present international tax system, it seems appropriate to view the FTC's turn to several of the stated core principles which indeed exceed mere bilateral concerns, notably sustainable development, fairness and human rights, through the prism of community interests. These core principles among those recalled in the FTC, are encompassed in the community interests Simma identifies in his seminal study.

Community interests can be identified by addressing concrete challenges, also in the realm of international taxation.[7] Bilateral approaches, primarily through DTAs and TIEAs, have tackled concrete challenges such as reducing double taxation and providing access to information, with varying degrees of success. Additionally, challenges including abusive transfer pricing, BEPS, and harmful tax competition, have prompted the G20 and OECD-led multilateral soft-law initiatives, treaty-based solutions, and coordinated domestic measures. Yet, Dagan observes it remains unclear whether these efforts genuinely promote a community interest, given uncertainty about what constitute community interests in international taxation.[8]

It can be argued that a functioning global tax system, even one primarily built on bilateral treaties, contributes to the community by upholding the rule of law, fostering certainty, and enhancing efficiency in international economic relations.[9] By mitigating double taxation, DTAs seem to support economic development—a critical component of sustainable development—while their procedural elements, such

[2] Simma (1994), p. 233; Feichtner (2012), para 2; Thin (2021), pp. 35, 55.

[3] Simma (1994), pp. 236–243.

[4] Simma (1994), p. 234.

[5] Feichtner (2012), para 4; Benvenisti and Nolte (2018), p. 5; Tietje and Lang (2018), p. 192 (This monograph is hereafter referred as 'Benvenisti and Nolte').

[6] Feichtner (2012), p. 18 (in relation to WTO law); As argue Stephen Schill and Vladislav Djanic in connection with investment agreements see 'International investment law and community interests' in Benvenisti and Nolte (2018), pp. 227–233; Tietje and Lang (2018), p. 220.

[7] Simma (1994), p. 233.

[8] Dagan (2018), p. 336.

[9] Feichtner (2012); Schill and Djanic (2018), pp. 227–233.

as fair dispute resolution with a minimum of due process, accountability, and prohibitions on tax discrimination, further align with community interests.[10]

Several of the principles proposed by the FTC can be associated with the notion of community interests as elaborated above. Given the 'common understanding' and 'common standard of achievement' of the Universal Declaration and the virtually complete coverage of the Covenants,[11] it is not in doubt that human rights are a concern of the international community as a whole rather than just one or more states.[12] Although it may be eternally debated what constitutes fairness in taxation,[13] it is undeniable that fairness or equity in the allocation of resources, often recognized by the Assembly[14] and in a variety of treaty norms,[15] is a core principle to the modern international legal order that is of concern to all. This is also reflected in the FTC's reference to 'the needs and capabilities of all countries, including LMICs and particularly countries in special situations', which evokes the Common But Different Responsibilities and Respective Capabilities (CBDR-RC) principle.[16] Furthermore, the FTC will refer to (legal) certainty in several instances, as a principle and as part of the objective ('certainty of international tax rules').[17] The SG Report emphasized that 'sufficient stability is required, such that businesses can reasonably plan for the long term'.[18] Alongside its explicit linkage to respect for human rights, it is noteworthy the SG Report and the relevant principle in the FTC shape this also as 'certainty *for taxpayers*' (emphasis added), which reflects that this is a principle protecting the interest of persons in the community, which underscore the FTC's alignment with the emerging significance of the individual in international law.[19]

---

[10] OECD (2017), arts 24, 25 and 26.

[11] International Covenant on Civil and Political Rights (adopted 16 December 1966, entered into force 23 March 1976) 999 UNTS 171 (ICCPR); International Covenant on Economic, Social and Cultural Rights (adopted 16 December 1966, entered into force 3 January 1976) 993 UNTS 3 (ICESCR).

[12] Preamble of the Universal Declaration of Human Rights, UNGA Res 217 (III) (10 December 1948) (adopted by 48 votes to none; 8 abstentions) (UDHR) [United Nations General Assembly (UNGA), 1948]. See also *Reservations to the Convention on Genocide* (Advisory Opinion) [1951] ICJ Rep 23 (*Reservations on Genocide*); *Application of the Convention on the Prevention and Punishment of the Crime of Genocide (The Gambia v Myanmar: 7 States intervening)* (Merits) [2022] ICJ Rep 477 (*Convention on Genocide*).

[13] Burgers and Mosquera Valderrama (2017), p. 767; Pirlot (2020b), p. 402.

[14] United Nations General Assembly (UNGA) (1974b) (1 May 1974); United Nations General Assembly (UNGA) (1974a) (12 December 1974); Franck (1998), pp. 2–24.

[15] Besson (2018), para 25.

[16] Rio Declaration (n 17 in Chap. 4) Principle 7; UNFCCC (n 39 in Chap. 2) art 3(1); Kyoto Protocol to the United Nations Framework Convention on Climate Change (adopted 11 December 1997, entered into force 16 February 2005) 2303 UNTS 162 (Kyoto Protocol) art 10.

[17] United Nations General Assembly (UNGA) (2024), para 9(h).

[18] United Nations General Assembly (UNGA) (2023a), para 12.

[19] Higgins (1999), pp. 78, 84–85.

This chapter will examine several of the core principles proposed by the FTC, which seem aligned with rise of community interests in public international law, notably sustainable development, fairness or equity and respect for human rights, and their potential significance for the shaping of the international tax system.

7.2 Sustainable Development

7.2.1 *Sustainable Development in the Framework Tax Convention*

With its Resolution 79/235, the UNGA has resolved that sustainable development will occupy a unique place in the FTC. It is the only term mentioned in the preamble,[20] the objectives,[21] in two of its guiding principles, and is the subject of at least one of the commitments.[22]

Resolution 78/230 on the FTC sets out to provide a new legal basis,[23] 'the establishment of an international tax system' aimed at ('for') sustainable development. Arguably, 'a new legal basis' reflects a conceptualization of the international tax system where tax measures are no longer exclusively governed by states' consent without any regard for the effect of its policies on other states, the nationals of those states, or the sustainable development of the community of nations.

7.2.2 *Sustainable Development and Its Present Interaction with Taxation*

The 1987 Brundtland Report provides one of the earliest modern definitions of sustainable development and remains widely cited. Sustainable development is defined as 'meeting the needs of the present without compromising the ability of future generations to meet their needs'.[24] In 1992, the Rio Declaration elaborated its components through 27 principles. Most directly relate to environmental protection.[25]

---

[20] Notably by referring to UNGA Res 70/1 [United Nations General Assembly (UNGA), 2015] on 'Transforming Our World: The 2030 Agenda for Sustainable Development', which is the key UN resolution on the Sustainable Development Goals (SDGs).

[21] United Nations General Assembly (UNGA) (2024), paras 9(d) and (f).

[22] Ibid, para 10(c).

[23] United Nations General Assembly (UNGA) (2023b), p. 2 ('establishing the legal basis for fully inclusive and more effective international tax cooperation').

[24] UN World Commission on Environment and Development (1987), p. 43; Lydgate (2012), pp. 621, 626 (who notes the failure of textualism with regard to sustainable development).

[25] Rio Declaration (n 17 in Chap. 4) Annex I.

These principles include the differentiation of obligations between HICs and LMICs, the principle that polluters should pay, the principle that preventing environmental damage is better than cleaning it up afterwards, the principle that environmental protection should be integrated with economic policy, and the right to development. Some note that a definition of sustainable development may be impossible or at least unnecessary: 'like justice or democracy, sustainable development may never be a "finished product". The determination of its substance will likely be a "continuing process", where a final definition is always beyond reach'.[26]

The dynamic evolution of the legal status of sustainable development is clearly discernible. Whereas Brownlie had to describe it as "problematic and nebulous" in 1998,[27] more than 20 years later Wolfrum was able to conclude that "the normative contours of the principle of sustainable development have developed clearly".[28] While not everyone agrees,[29] sustainable development is widely seen as comprising[30] or at least closely related to principles constituting generally applicable rules of international law in their own right. For example, the duty to prevent significant environmental harm and to respect the environment of other states, closely connected to sustainable development,[31] is clearly part of general international law.[32] The duty upon states to act with due diligence in connection with the environment, which is closely related to sustainable development,[33] is customary international law.[34] Similarly, it has been noted that sustainable development is further elaborated

[26] Voigt (2009), p. 165.

[27] Brownlie (1998), p. 287.

[28] Wolfrum (2019), p. 163. See also Voigt (2009), p. 154. See also United Nations General Assembly (UNGA) (2015), p. 1.

[29] Beyerlin and Marauhn (2011), p. 81.

[30] Birnie et al. (2009), p. 116.

[31] United Nations (1972) (Stockholm Declaration), Principle 21; United Nations (1992) (Rio Declaration), Principle 2.

[32] *Trail Smelter Arbitration* (Award of 16 April 1938 and 11 March 1941) [1941] UNRIAA 1905, 1965; *Corfu Channel (United Kingdom of Great Britain and Northern Ireland v Albania)* (Merits) [1949] ICJ Rep 4, 22 (*Corfu Channel*); *Legality of the Threat or Use of Nuclear Weapons* (Advisory Opinion) [1996] ICJ Rep 226 (*Legality of the Threat or Use of Nuclear Weapons*), para 29; *Dispute over the Status and Use of the Waters of the Silala (Chile v Bolivia)* (Merits) [2022] ICJ Rep 614 (*Waters of the Silala*), paras 83 and 99.

[33] See for example Rio Declaration (n 17 in Chap. 4) Principles 2, 4, 11, 13, 17.

[34] *Pulp Mills on the River Uruguay (Argentina v Uruguay)* (Merits) [2010] ICJ Rep 14 (*Pulp Mills*), para 197. *Request for an Advisory Opinion Submitted by the Commission of Small Island States on Climate Change and International Law* (Advisory Opinion of 21 May 2024), ITLOS Case No 31, ITLOS Reports 2024 available at <https://www.itlos.org/fileadmin/itlos/documents/cases/31/Advisory_Opinion/C31_Adv_Op_21.05.2024_corr.pdf> last accessed 29 July 2025 (ITLOS *Climate Change Advisory Opinion*), para 235.

in the precautionary principle,[35] "an integral part of the general obligation of due diligence".[36]

The International Court of Justice (ICJ) has referred to sustainable development in several of its decisions. In the 1996 Advisory Opinion on the Legality of the Threat of Nuclear Weapons, the ICJ referred to Article 24 of the Rio Declaration, which stated that States have a duty to protect the environment, even in the case of armed conflict.[37] In the 1997 Gabčíkovo–Nagymaros case, centred around the question if a controversial dam on the Donau river should be completed, the relevant treaties did not mention sustainable development, but both Hungary and Slovakia had invoked it.[38]

The ICJ considered that, although in the past economic development had proceeded without considering the effects on the environment, 'new norms and standards have to be taken into consideration and given proper weight […] This need to reconcile economic development with protection of the environment is aptly expressed in the concept of sustainable development'.[39] In the Iron Rhine arbitration in 2005, the Tribunal explicitly asserted that the duty to mitigate environmental harm in the case of economic development is indeed a principle of general international law and then used it to interpret an 1839 treaty between Belgium and the Netherlands[40] as per Article 31 (3) (c) of the Vienna Convention Law of Treaties.[41] In 2008, in the Pulp Mills case, the ICJ recognised the principle of prevention as part of customary international law.[42] In its advisory opinion on climate change, the ICJ, citing the 'continuous and uncontested universal recognition' of sustainable development, elevated its status from a mere concept—as articulated in the *Gabčíkovo–Nagymaros* case nearly three decades ago—to an applicable legal

[35] New Delhi Declaration (n 16 in Chap. 4); Schrijver (2008), p. 340.

[36] *Responsibilities and obligations of States sponsoring persons and entities with respect to activities in the Area (No 17)* (Advisory Opinion of 1 February 2011) ITLOS Reports 2011 (ITLOS *Area Advisory Opinion*), para 131.

[37] Rio Declaration (n 17 in Chap. 4) art. 24: 'Warfare is inherently destructive of sustainable development. States shall therefore respect international law providing protection for the environment in times of armed conflict and cooperate in its further development, as necessary'; See also *Legality of the Threat of Nuclear Weapons* (Advisory Opinion) [1996] ICJ Rep 226, para 27.

[38] *Gabčíkovo-Nagymaros* (n 19 in Chap. 4).

[39] ibid, para 140.

[40] Treaty between the Kingdom of the Netherlands and the Kingdom of Belgium concerning the separation of the respective territories (adopted 19 April 1839, entered into force 8 June 1839), Tractatenblad [1955] 157.

[41] *Arbitration regarding the Iron Rhine ("Ijzeren Rijn") Railway between the Kingdom of Belgium and the Kingdom of the Netherlands* (Decision of 24 May 2005) v. XXVII RIAA pp. 35–125, para 59 (Iron Rhine Decision); VCLT (n 1 in Chap. 4).

[42] *Pulp Mills on the River Uruguay (Argentina v. Uruguay)* (Judgment) [2010] ICJ Reports 14, para 101.

principle.[43] This elevation reflects its progressive development as a source of law,[44] significantly influenced by its emergence as a treaty norm in recent years.[45]

The three 'dimensions' to sustainable development formulated at the 2005 World Summit, environmental, economic, and social, are also reflected in the FTC:

> [Efforts to achieve the objectives of the framework convention therefore should] take a holistic, sustainable development perspective that covers in a balanced and integrated manner economic, social and environmental policy aspects.[46]

At roughly the same time the UN formulated its 17 SDGs with 169 associated targets, with several targets that are not relate directly to the environment,[47] the question of financing through taxation was reflected in the Addis Agenda, which is also referenced in the FTC.[48]

Now several decades following its initial framing,[49] sustainable development has appeared by and in itself as a treaty norm not only in environmental treaties[50] but also in the Treaty of Maastricht of the EU,[51] the Charter of Fundamental Rights of the European Union,[52] and various trade and investment agreements.[53] As a norm of

---

[43] International Court of Justice (ICJ) (2025), para 147; *Gabčíkovo-Nagymaros* (n 19 in Chap. 4), para 140. Just prior to that, in *Legality of the Threat or Use of Nuclear Weapons* (n 32 in this chapter); Sands (1999), pp. 389, 399; Voigt (2009), p. 165; *Gabčíkovo-Nagymaros* (n 19 in Chap. 4) Separate Opinion of Vice-President Weeramantry [1997] ICJ Rep 88.

[44] Wolfrum (2019); Weiss (2019b), p. 177; Barral (2012), pp. 377–400; Voigt (2009), p. 165; Schrijver (2008), pp. 288–317; Sands et al. (2012), p. 206; see also in general: Boyle and Freestone (1999); French (2005); Ramlogan (2011).

[45] For example, Paris Agreement (n 10 in Chap. 5) art 4; Treaty on European Union (signed 7 February 1992, entered into force 1 November 1993) 1757 UNTS 3 (Treaty on European Union); Charter of the Fundamental Rights of the European Union (entered into force 1 December 2000) OJ 2012/C 326/02 (EU Charter) art 37; United Nations (2003); EU—Free Trade Agreement between the European Union and its Member States, of the one part, and the Republic of Korea, of the other part (adopted 6 October 2010, entered into force 13 December 2015) OJ L127 (EU—Korea FTA) chapter 13; Trade and Cooperation Agreement between the European Union and the European Atomic Energy Community, of the one part, and the United Kingdom of Great Britain and Northern Ireland, of the other part (signed 30 December 2020, entered into force 1 May 2021) OJ L149/10 (TCA) title XI.

[46] United Nations General Assembly (UNGA) (2024), art 9(d); see also United Nations General Assembly (UNGA) (2005), para 48.

[47] United Nations General Assembly (UNGA) (2015).

[48] United Nations General Assembly (UNGA) (2024), art 6(d).

[49] Brundtland (1987).

[50] Paris Agreement (n 10 in Chap. 5) art 4. For example, the Cooperation Agreement between the European Community and the Lao People's Democratic Republic (signed 29 April 1997, entered into force 1 December 1997) 2003 UNTS 3, which imposes parties to effectively implement environmental laws and regulations. See Schrijver (2008), pp. 288–317.

[51] Treaty on European Union (n 45 in this chapter); see sustainable development in EU law in general in Van Hees (2014), p. 60.

[52] EU Charter (n 45 in this chapter) art 37.

[53] Korea FTA (n 45 in this chapter) chapter 13; TCA (n 45 in this chapter) title XI; United States—Mexico—Canada Agreement (signed 30 November 2018, entered into force 1 July 2020) 32 ILM 289 (USMCA).

a treaty that is binding between two states, there is no reason why sustainable development should somehow not *a priori* constitute an applicable rule (and not just a concept[54]) for a DTA between these same states. But, as a treaty norm and otherwise, sustainable development is "complex and multi-faceted"[55] and even today it lacks a widely agreed detailed definition.[56]

To determine its legal significance, in this case to international taxation, one may approach sustainable development as one single principle[57] but also as a complex compound of principles, goals and concepts where the status as a source of international law may depend on each component.[58] One or more of its components may constitute or overlap a general principle of international law or rules of customary international law in their own right. For example, in *Pulp Mills*, the ICJ recognised the principle of prevention as part of customary international law.[59] In *Corfu Channel*, the ICJ recognised a duty of due diligence under general international law as 'every State's obligation not to allow knowingly its territory to be used for acts contrary to the rights of other States'.[60] In *Silala* the ICJ referred to 'the customary obligation to prevent transboundary harm'.[61] In the *Iron Rhine* arbitration in 2005, the Tribunal explicitly asserted that the duty to mitigate environmental harm in the case of economic development is indeed a principle of general international law and then used it to interpret an 1839 treaty between Belgium and the Netherlands[62] as per Article 31 (3) (c) of the Vienna Convention on the Law of Treaties (VCLT).[63] Norms like these are often understood to be components of sustainable development,[64] while they have also developed into binding rules of general international law in their own right.

Broad and multifaceted as it is,[65] sustainable development has previously been associated with (international) taxation in numerous ways.[66] Taxation is indirectly connected to every SDG as a means of financing. The SG Report which set up the vote on the FTC in resolution 78/230 noted that inclusive and effective international

---

[54] *Gabčíkovo-Nagymaros* (n 19 in Chap. 4).

[55] Schrijver (2008), p. 366.

[56] Weiss (2019a), p. 175.

[57] Persson et al. (2016), pp. 59, 63.

[58] Schrijver (2008), pp. 339–362; New Delhi Declaration (n 16 in Chap. 4) 22; Atapattu (2019), pp. 215, 237; Wolfrum (2019), p. 163.

[59] *Pulp Mills* (n 34 in this chapter), para 101; *Legality of the Threat or Use of Nuclear Weapons* (n 32 in this chapter), para 29.

[60] *Corfu Channel* (n 32 in this chapter) 22.

[61] *Waters of the Silala* (n 32 in this chapter), paras 83 and 99.

[62] Tractatenblad (n 40 in this chapter) 157.

[63] *Iron Rhine (Belgium v Netherlands)*, PCA Case No 2003-02, Award (24 May 2005), para 59; VCLT (n 1 in Chap. 4).

[64] Schrijver (2008), pp. 333–339.

[65] Ibid 366.

[66] Pirlot (2020a); Gribnau and Jallai (2018).

tax cooperation, in terms of substance, should cover, among other things, the fact that international tax rules should strengthen the ability of LMICs to finance their SDGs.[67] In this regard, a frequent point of discussion between HICs and LMICs is how the latter can increase their financial self-reliance, reflected in the concept of DRM.[68] This was explored in detail as part of the Addis Ababa Action Agenda of 2015,[69] and shortly afterwards is referred in the SDGs as part of Goal 17.[70] At the Ad Hoc Committee, especially high-income countries emphasised that DRM, which overlaps with IFFs[71] and capacity building,[72] should play an important role in the FTC.[73] The financing role of taxation for sustainable development as linked to global taxing rights, is one of the main drivers of the FTC:

> [T]he changes being developed through [the OECD two pillar solution] would not fully address a broader discontent rooted in the long-standing conviction, held by many countries [...] that existing tax treaty rules do not reserve sufficient taxing rights for countries hosting multinational enterprises and constituting markets for their products.[74]

Furthermore, a tax measure may directly impact sustainable development, either positively or negatively.[75] An obvious example is the role of Pigouvian taxation in climate change mitigation, where it operates primarily as one of only a few possible ways to 'price' the carbon content of fossil fuels and other products in accordance with their adverse environmental impacts.[76] Taxes may constitute 'domestic mitigation measures' in the sense of the Paris Agreement for a state to reach its Nationally Determined Contributions (NDCs).[77] A similar direct link between tax and sustainable development is found in the Framework Convention on Tobacco Control (FCTC).[78] The FCTC provides that 'each Party may, as appropriate, implement tax policies on tobacco to contribute to health objectives, and restrict import of tax- and duty-free tobacco products'.[79] The FCTC has created a reporting system for parties

---

[67] United Nations General Assembly (UNGA) (2023a), paras 10–18.

[68] Schrijver (2008), p. 280; See also Hongler (2021), pp. 13–14 (noting that taxes have become part of a broader sustainability debate, and pointing out the connection with DMR).

[69] United Nations (2015), para 53.

[70] United Nations General Assembly (UNGA) (2015), goal 17.1.

[71] United Nations General Assembly (UNGA) (2024), paras 10(b) and (e).

[72] United Nations General Assembly (UNGA) (2024), paras 11 and 12; Meyer-Nandi (2021), pp. 63–64.

[73] For example in the statement dated 29 July 2024 by the European Union, proposing that commitments should be on a complementary basis: European Union, Inputs to the Second Session (n 44 in Chap. 2); Germany, Inputs to the Second Session (n 44 in Chap. 2); Singapore, Inputs to the Second Session (n 44 in Chap. 2); United States, Inputs to the Second Session (n 44 in Chap. 2).

[74] United Nations General Assembly (UNGA) (2023a), para 5.

[75] Hongler (2021), pp. 13–14.

[76] Taxes that are mainly meant to influence behaviour rather than raise revenue for the state; Pigou (1920).

[77] Paris Agreement (n 10 in Chap. 5) arts 3, 4.

[78] FCTC (n 1 in Chap. 4) art 6(2).

[79] Ibid art 6(2).

to increase transparency on tobacco-related taxes that is backed up by soft law guidelines.[80] During the preparation of the TOR for the FTC, a significant number of states expressed that the FTC should play a role in environmental taxation in general, or specifically carbon taxes.[81]

Both these dimensions of 'an international tax system for sustainable development', i.e. direct and indirectly as financing, are reflected in Resolution 79/235, which has positioned sustainable development as a cornerstone of the FTC, embedding it within the preamble,[82] objectives,[83] two guiding principles, and at least one of the commitments.[84] As a direct means to impact SDGs sustainable environmental taxation was frequently highlighted at the TOR Committee.[85] France, for instance, noted the UN's central role not only in addressing climate change and marine environmental conservation but also in regulating greenhouse gas (GHG) emissions from shipping through the International Maritime Organization (IMO) and international aviation through the International Civil Aviation Organization (ICAO).[86] This underscores the UN's suitability as a forum for tackling GHG emissions in these sectors through international tax cooperation.

The FTC underscores the role of tax policy in indirectly financing SDGs, including climate change objectives. The SG Report frames this ambition as enabling countries in exercising their taxing rights, mobilising resources to invest in the SDGs and climate action while also promoting fiscal policies that are aligned with the SDGs.[87] This alignment of international tax cooperation with the advancement of the SDGs garnered support at the TOR Committee with LMICs and some HICs endorsing its inclusion.[88] The significance of national and international tax systems as a crucial general financing mechanism for climate objectives is highlighted in the

---

[80] WHO Framework Convention on Tobacco Control (2017).

[81] In the written submissions of the First Session (n 44 in Chap. 2): Chile, Colombia, Kenya, Russia, The Bahamas, Pakistan, and the ATAF, as well as HICs The Netherlands, Norway, Italy and France. In the written inputs to the Second Session (n 44 in Chap. 2): Kenya, Canada/Australia/New Zealand, France, The Netherlands, Spain, The Philippines, Sweden, Russia and Tanzania.

[82] Notably by referring to UNGA Res 70/1 [United Nations General Assembly (UNGA), 2015] on 'Transforming our world: the 2030 agenda for sustainable development'.

[83] United Nations General Assembly (UNGA) (2024), arts 9(d), (f).

[84] United Nations General Assembly (UNGA) (2024), art 10(c).

[85] Written inputs First Session (n 44 in Chap. 2) by several states mentioning that environmental taxation would be an appropriate area of international cooperation under the FTC including Chile, Colombia, Kenya, Russia, The Bahamas, Pakistan, and the ATAF, as well as HICs The Netherlands, Norway, Italy, and France. In the written inputs Second Session (n 44 in Chap. 2) a number of states specifically mentioned possible cooperation on environmental taxes, including Kenya, Canada/Australia/New Zealand, France, The Netherlands, Spain, The Philippines, Sweden, Russia, and Tanzania; similarly Brazil, verbal statement First Session, 6th Meeting (n 44 in Chap. 2).

[86] Written inputs First Session (n 44 in Chap. 2) by France.

[87] United Nations General Assembly (UNGA) (2023a), para 11.

[88] Including Written inputs First Session (n 44 in Chap. 2) by Nigeria, ATAF, Spain, Switzerland, Sweden, Slovenia, Slovakia, Columbia, Denmark, Japan; and to Second session (n 44 in Chap. 2) by African Group, China, The Netherlands, Norway.

analysis of UN treaty bodies and experts,[89] underscoring the role of the FTC in this respect:

> This global tax deal [the FTC] is needed to end the exploitation of the public purse and the environment by multinational corporations, the ultra-rich, and polluters. [...] Ultimately, tax justice and climate justice are deeply interconnected.[90]

The claim that international tax rules obstruct LMICs' ability to fund SDGs, which is closely related to the allegation that taxing rights are unfairly established needs to be nuanced, and this is undertaken in the next section. However, it should be emphasized that even if accurate, reallocating taxing rights to any state or group of states does not inherently ensure that such funds will be allocated to financing sustainable development, underscoring a critical disconnect between tax revenue generation and policy outcomes.[91]

7.2.3 An International Tax System Aimed at and Guided by Sustainable Development

Sustainable development has attained a position of considerable influence -in the words of Judge Higgins- 'at the heart of international law'.[92] As an objective and a principle, sustainable development is in a position to give direction to the parties to create new commitments under the FTC and in protocols.[93] It seems that environmental taxation may be one of the best examples of that. This was also observed at the Ad Hoc Committee.[94] As is well-known, the Kyoto Protocol placed responsibility to drive the reduction of global aviation emissions with the ICAO, which indeed created the (voluntary) Carbon Offsetting and Reduction Scheme for International

---

[89] United Nations General Assembly (UNGA) Human Rights Council (2025) (pursuant to Human Rights Council resolution 52/17) (UN Doc A/HRC/58/51); see also the recent Statement: Committee on Economic, Social and Cultural Rights (CESCR) (2021).

[90] UN Doc A/HRC/58/51 (n 89 in this chapter), paras 44–45.

[91] Stark (2022), p. 133.

[92] Higgins (1995), p. 17.

[93] On the difference between a principle and a rule, and normative detail see *North Sea Continental Shelf (Germany v Netherlands/Denmark)* (Merits) [1969] ICJ Rep 3 (*North Sea Continental Shelf*), para 74.

[94] In the written submissions of the First Session (n 44 in Chap. 2), several states made a point of mentioning that environmental taxation would be an appropriate area of international cooperation under the UNFCTC including Chile, Colombia, Kenya, Russia, The Bahamas, Pakistan, and the ATAF, as well as HICs The Netherlands, Norway, Italy, and France. In the inputs to the Second Session (n 44 in Chap. 2) a number of states specifically mentioned possible cooperation on environmental taxes, including Kenya, Canada/Australia/New Zealand, France, The Netherlands, Spain, The Philippines, Sweden, Russia, and Tanzania; Brazil, 6th Meeting of the First Session (30 April 2024) (n 44 in Chap. 2).

Aviation (CORSIA) initiative[95] However, ever since the Chicago Convention, aviation treaties and ICAO recommendations have ensured various tax exemptions, including taxes on certain fuel, and these are still in place.[96] Progress on the environmental pricing of shipping fuel, including through a carbon tax, has been problematic as well.[97] It requires an international approach to be effective because vessels might just take on fuel in markets that impose lower taxes on fuel.[98] There is an increased awareness that something must be done in these areas, as reflected in a new EU Energy Tax Directive[99] and a "task force on international taxation" launched by several states regarding to focus on global taxes on fuel for international aviation and shipping.[100]

This growing awareness comes at a time the UN will be given a new tool i.e. a protocol under the FTC regarding environmental challenges.[101] As was mentioned by France at the Ad Hoc Committee,[102] occupying the central institutional position not only on climate change and environmental conservation on the seas, but also on shipping through the IMO and international aviation through the ICAO, it is hard to deny the UN might be the best placed forum to address GHG emissions by shipping and aviation.

7.3 Fairness or Equity

The established principle that international taxation should be fair and equitable, long recognized, centrally guides the FTC's proposed framework for international tax relationships.[103] The ICJ's jurisprudence underscores that equity is not just a broad societal aim, but also constitutes a legal principle, and regards it as part of the applicable law in relation to climate change.[104] As a legal principle, it is underscored

---

[95] Kyoto Protocol (n 16 in this chapter) art 2(2); International Civil Aviation Organization (ICAO) (2016).

[96] Convention on International Civil Aviation (signed 7 December 1944, entered into force 4 April 1947) 15 UNTS 295 (Chicago Convention) art 24; ICAO (1993).

[97] Parry et al. (2018), p. 5; Black et al. (2024), p. 11.

[98] Faber et al. (2022).

[99] European Union (EU) (2021); Council Directive (EC) 2003/96/EC of 27 October 2003, European Union (EU) (2003).

[100] Global Solidarity Levies Task Force (n.d.).

[101] United Nations General Assembly (UNGA) (2024), paras 15–17.

[102] France, Inputs to the First Session (n 44 in Chap. 2).

[103] Henry (2016), p. 43; Brock and Pogge (2014), p. 1; Avi-Yonah (2016), p. 137; International Bar Association (2013); OECD (2009).

[104] International Court of Justice (ICJ) (2025), paras 152–154.

by several decisions and opinions,[105] and incorporated in a large number of treaty regimes.[106]

For the FTC, Resolution 79/235 establishes that fairness or equity occupies a significant position. The stated objective of the FTC is to establish an inclusive international tax system that is, among other things, 'fair' and 'equitable' with a view of 'enhancing the fairness of international tax rules'. It also states that the FTC's principles will include 'sufficient flexibility to ensure equitable results as societies and technology evolves. and ensures 'fairness in allocation of international taxing rights', a notion that is repeated in the commitments as Resolution 79/235 prescribes 'equitable taxation of multinational enterprises'.

In the discussions on the FTC at the UN, fairness or equity was explored along several contentious issues in international tax relationships. Mainly, the debates highlighted the issue of equitable international taxing rights, fairness as it relates to harmful special tax regimes, an equitable inclusion of all states in global tax governance. In addition, this chapter examines the implications of equity from the standpoint of domestic tax policies.

7.3.1 Fair International Taxing Rights

Principles of fairness or equity have long been invoked to address economic disparities within the international tax system, with debates often centring on the equitable distribution of taxing rights between HICs and LMICs. Indeed, as Brown-Weiss observes, 'frequently we turn to a norm of equity to address economic disparity'.[107]

In relation to international taxation these discussions, rooted in historical tensions such as the '1920s compromise' on taxing rights, have gained prominence in calls for a 'globally fair, sustainable, and modern international tax system'.[108] The balance of taxing rights, primarily shaped by OECD modelled DTAs (with some deviations in the UN Model Tax Convention) and the OECD TPG governing certain cross-border aspects of income tax, has been criticised for favouring HICs.[109] Such

---

[105] *North Sea Continental Shelf* (n 93 in this chapter), para 85; *Continental Shelf (Tunisia/Libyan Arab Jamahiriya)* [1982] ICJ Rep 18 (*Continental Shelf*), para 71; *Loan Agreement between Italy and Costa Rica (Dispute Arising under a Financing Agreement)* (1998) 25 RIAA 23 (*Loan Agreement*), para 69; *Factory at Chorzów (Germany v Poland)* (Merits) PCIJ Rep Series A No 17; *Nuclear Tests (Australia v France)* (Merits) [1974] ICJ Rep 253, 268; *Temple of Preah Vihear (Cambodia v Thailand)* (Merits) [1962] ICJ Rep 6; *North Sea Continental Shelf* (n 93 in this chapter). See also Rosenne (1988), pp. 85, 88–89; Jennings (1986), pp. 27, 35; Franck (1998), p. 151.

[106] UNFCCC (n 39 in Chap. 2) art 3(1); Kyoto Protocol (n 16 in this chapter) art 10; GATT (n 5 in Chap. 5) arts XVIII, XXXVI; United Nations Convention on the Law of the Sea (signed 10 December 1982, entered into force 16 November 1994) 1833 UNTS 397 (UNCLOS) Preamble and arts 74, 83.

[107] Weiss (2019a).

[108] Group of Twenty (G20) (2023), para 62.

[109] Graetz (1991), pp. 261, 262; Ozai (2020), pp. 317, 324; Brooks and Krever (2015), pp. 159, 166.

argument is often based on the primacy of residence to assign taxing rights under DTAs, and on the way transfer pricing rules assign taxable value to skills, capital and IP which are more likely to be found in HICs than in LMICs. Scholars, such as Devereux and Vella, argue that the '1920s compromise'—balancing residence and source taxation—is outdated and 'wholly inappropriate for taxing modern multinational companies'.[110] In fact, the 'éminence grise' of international taxation, Klaus Vogel, admitted as early as 1988 that the system was 'unjust and detrimental' to states disadvantaged by its structure.[111]

The discourse on fairness in international taxation extends beyond technical rules to broader questions of global justice. Ozai defines fairness in the international tax system as 'the equitable and balanced allocation of taxing rights, resources, and responsibilities among states', arguing that rules should neither disproportionately favour wealthier nations nor disadvantage less developed ones.[112] Dagan asserts that the legitimacy of the international tax regime hinges on its ability to deliver justice for less well-off states.[113] Pogge and others note that reallocating taxing rights to allow LMICs to tax multinationals at source or curb offshore asset concealment could mobilise resources to reduce poverty and fund human rights protections, though he admits this depends on states' domestic allocation decisions.[114] Indeed, Stark cautions that 'the reallocation from state to state does not necessarily help when it comes to fulfilling duties of justice towards individuals',[115] highlighting the gap between systemic reform and tangible outcomes for individuals.

Turning to the FTC, the SG Report focused on the "broader discontent rooted in the long-standing conviction by many countries and stakeholders that the existing tax treaty rules do not reserve sufficient taxing rights to countries hosting multinational enterprises and constituting markets for their products".[116] In the FTC context, the digital economy and technological development in general is thought to exasperate the problem of taxing rights, for example as the lack of physical presence may prevent source states from levying income tax under tax treaties.[117] As India put it:

> In the digital economy, developing countries are often left at a disadvantage, as they struggle to tax services provided by foreign companies that do not have a physical presence within their borders.[118]

Brazil proposed at the TOR Committee to include provisions for revenue-sharing agreements among states, ensuring that digital taxes collected in one jurisdiction are

[110] Devereux and Vella (2014); along the same lines: Faccio and Ghosh (2024), p. 358.

[111] Vogel (1988).

[112] Ozai (2025), p. 642.

[113] Dagan (2017), p. 34.

[114] Pogge and Mehtha (2016), p. 43.

[115] Stark (2022), p. 160.

[116] United Nations General Assembly (UNGA) (2023a), para 5.

[117] United Nations General Assembly (UNGA) (2023a), paras 12, 24.

[118] Verbal statements First Session (3rd meeting) (n 44 in Chap. 2) by India.

fairly distributed among the countries where economic activity occurs.[119] As was mentioned, the OECD's Pillar One tried to reallocate taxing rights over the digital economy, but as the SG Report set out,[120] some LMICs have expressed dissatisfaction with the proposed reforms and presently progress seems to have stalled.

Presumptions underpinning the FTC about the unfavourable distribution of taxing rights for LMICs, particularly by means of DTAs, may be largely accurate in the abstract. However, in practice a more nuanced examination is required to assess its actual impact on the tax revenues of LMICs. DTAs represent a limited source of international obligations restricting the taxing rights of states. While applicable to income tax, and for example not to VAT/GST, sales taxes and excises, they do not restrict corporate income tax on the profit of foreign invested enterprises that are locally established. Practically speaking, in terms of business taxation, DTAs mostly reduce withholding taxes on dividend, interest and royalties (and sometimes services) and exempt business income derived without a local permanent establishment, an exemption that has starkly eroded in recent decades even in its OECD format. DTAs leave LMICs largely unfettered autonomy to design and implement domestic tax policies. The states can, generally without any interference from DTAs, set corporate income tax rates, restrict the tax deductibility of expenses, levy VAT on cross-border transactions, impose new levies (such as DSTs that are not income taxes), impose procedural requirements, eliminate tax holidays, conduct tax audits and issue transfer pricing reassessments. LMICs can set their own anti-avoidance, anti-erosion or thin capitalization standards mostly unchecked by DTAs, and the above-mentioned primacy of residence-based taxation is in practice for most investments overtaken by a regulatory requirement in LMICs to establish a local subsidiary. While it is accurate that some tax authorities in LMICs lack expertise and access to information in the context of auditing multinationals and transfer pricing assessments, this shortfall can equally manifest as the imposition of excessive tax burdens or the failure to accurately assess a fair share of taxes. Ultimately, DTAs have limited impact on the power tax agencies wield over taxpayers, as domestic courts—except in rare instances—retain final jurisdiction over all tax impositions, including assessments that may contravene the provisions of a DTA. Typically, although situations may differ from state to state, domestic taxable resources via VAT, excise, and income taxes on resident individuals and companies far exceed the few cross-border tax imposts which are directly affected by DTAs (mainly withholding taxes). Anyway, LMICs can and frequently do renegotiate or terminate DTAs to address perceived imbalances.[121]

---

119 Verbal statements First Session (11th meeting) (n 44 in Chap. 2) by Brazil.

120 United Nations General Assembly (UNGA) (2023a), para 36.

121 Vanderbruggen (2002), № 7/8.

7.3.2 *The Unfairness of Harmful Special Tax Regimes*

Tax competition represents a significant concern within the international tax system, often framed as an issue of fairness with divergent perspectives. While curbing tax incentive regimes is one of the key elements of the OECD and G20 BEPS project, some smaller states and certain LMICs may view their tax incentives as legitimate tools to attract investment, perceiving countermeasures as unfair restrictions on their economic strategies. As was mentioned above, this tension was underscored in the SG Report, which highlighted the challenges posed by such competing interests.[122] The African Group, in discussions prior to the First Session of the TOR Committee, advocated for addressing 'harmful tax regimes' as a key commitment and a priority for early protocols.[123] Reflecting this, the TOR includes 'harmful tax practices' as a proposed commitment, signalling a focus on mitigating practices that exacerbate global tax inequities.[124]

The *Micula v Romania* case, a notable investor-state dispute settlement (ISDS) claim, arose when Romania's withdrawal of a tax holiday prompted a 2013 tribunal award of €120 million in favour of the investor.[125] The European Commission deemed the payment of damages as a circumvention of State aid rules, triggering further litigation. Although the General Court initially ruled in favour of the investor, the Court of Justice of the European Union (CJEU) determined in 2020 that the payment of the 2013 award constituted State aid, given that it was issued after Romania's accession to the EU.[126] The enforcement dispute remains unresolved.[127]

Consequently, there is no apparent universal consensus beyond the IF regarding whether states should refrain from implementing tax incentives that could adversely affect other states, or indeed from offering any tax incentives whatsoever. Conversely, given that anti-tax haven measures have been incorporated into domestic tax legislation for nearly as long as tax havens have existed, there appears to be a shared understanding that states are entitled to adopt domestic tax measures to counter such incentives (such as anti-avoidance measures, or a 'top-up tax' on the group's top company to compensate for lack of taxes overseas). While many LMICs agree

[122] See above Sect. 6.5; United Nations General Assembly (UNGA) (2023a), para 38.

[123] Written inputs First session (n 44 in Chap. 2) Nigeria (on behalf of the African Group) items 6, 7.

[124] United Nations General Assembly (UNGA) (2024), para 10(e); see also United Nations (2015), para 27.

[125] As the Commission wrote in 2015 (initiated in 2005, arbitration award in 2013), in all but name referring to this case: European Commission (2015), p. 5; Keller (2023), p. 159, para 40.

[126] Commission Decision (EU) 2015/1470 of 30 March 2015 on State aid SA.38517 (2014/C) (ex 2014/NN) implemented by Romania—Arbitral award Micula v Romania of 11 December 2013 [European Union (EU), 2013]; Cases T-624/15, T-694/15 and T-704/15 *European Food SA and Others v European Commission* EU:T:2019:423; Case C-638/19 P *European Commission v European Food SA and Others* ECLI:EU:C:2022:50. The enforcement of the award is an ongoing battle. See for example Case C-516/22 *European Commission v United Kingdom of Great Britain and Northern Ireland* ECLI:EU:C:2024:231.

[127] For an overview of developments: Sorace (2024).

with the IF's approach (approximately one third of the IF is comprised of LMICs) and about a dozen LMICs have at the time of writing abolished or adjusted at least some of their tax incentive regimes,[128] the SG Report nevertheless points out that 'tax incentives can be used to attract investment'.[129] Several LMICs UN Members at the TOR Committee suggested that some tax incentives are legitimate and appropriate, for example to compensate for a small market or lack of resources.[130]

7.3.3 Inclusive Global Tax Governance

A significant impetus for the FTC is the perceived lack of participatory fairness in global tax governance, particularly the exclusion of many LMICs from decision-making processes. The SG Report indicated that, at the time of its publication, 67 UN Members were excluded from policy-making within the IF,[131] Additional barriers, such as limited resources, the complexity of tax rules, time constraints, insufficient technical expertise, and certain preconditions for participation, further hindered effective involvement of LMICs.[132] The Chair of the TOR Committee, in opening remarks, cautioned against 'allowing a few states or organizations to dictate their rules'.[133] This sentiment was echoed by Brazil, which stated: 'for too long, the voices of developing countries have been sidelined in international tax discussions'.[134] These concerns underscore the FTC's aim to foster a more inclusive framework for international tax cooperation, ensuring broader participation in shaping global tax policies. Criticism extended beyond the limited membership, but also concerned restrictive membership conditions (e.g. committing to implement mandatory minimum standards in the BEPS framework), and outcomes misaligned with LMIC priorities or costly to implement as noted in the SG Report and TOR Committee discussions.[135]

Whilst these participatory concerns are valid, they obscure deeper disagreements. The lack of full consensus underscores the challenge of achieving universal agreement in a larger, more diverse forum like the UN.[136] The larger the group, the

[128] OECD (2021), pp. 18, 25.

[129] United Nations General Assembly (UNGA) (2023a), para 38.

[130] For example Verbal statements First Session (n 44 in Chap. 2): The Bahamas, Sri Lanka (6th meeting) and Nigeria (7th meeting); Verbal statements Second session (n 44 in Chap. 2): Jamaica (4th meeting). See also United Nations (2015), para 27; see also Parada (2025), pp. 188, 210.

[131] United Nations General Assembly (UNGA) (2023a), para 34.

[132] United Nations General Assembly (UNGA) (2023a), para 39; Christensen et al. (2020).

[133] Verbal statements First Session (n 44 in Chap. 2) Chair opening remarks (1st Meeting).

[134] Verbal statements First Session (n 44 in Chap. 2) Brazil (4th meeting) and Jamaica (1st Meeting).

[135] United Nations General Assembly (UNGA) (2023a), para 41–43.

[136] The OECD points out that the Inclusive Framework covers more than 90% of global GDP: OECD (2023).

harder the consensus.[137] It is not uncommon that ad hoc formulas facilitate a better participation.[138] A less than universal consensus does not and should not exclude plurilateral progress.[139]

7.3.4 *Fairness in Domestic Tax Policy*

The domestic dimension of taxation has been a focus at the TOR Committee, with HICs particularly emphasizing its importance. At the TOR Committee, HICs repeatedly raised the FTC should also address problems in national tax systems, such as lack of transparency, a narrow tax base and lack of capacity.[140] The EU, in a common statement, had suggested to include DRM, capacity building and fostering tax compliance as commitments,[141] as did Germany.[142] Singapore proposed to make DRM into an early protocol, but instead the TOR Committee chose to include DRM into the FTC's objective.[143] The US criticized the FTC only mentions DRM 'in such a way that little importance is placed on it'.[144]

Challenges to DRM have earlier been highlighted as the UN, as part of the Addis Ababa Action Agenda, and other institutions highlighted the need to enhance the fairness of Members' tax systems by measures such as 'broadening the tax base'.[145] A lack of progressivity is at times flagged in the output of UN human rights treaty bodies, as is examined in detail in the next section of this chapter.[146] The effective taxation of affluent individuals in LMICs is often impeded by enforcement difficulties.[147]

A G20 note prepared by the IMF staff cited by HICs at the TOR Committee concluded that domestic tax reforms—such as reducing tax incentives, enhancing VAT, curbing non-compliance, and improving administration—could yield significantly more revenue than certain international tax cooperation measures.[148] Ongoing international tax cooperation make a 'positive but modest revenue contribution' while there is 'significant scope for revenue mobilization through domestic tax

137 Stewart (2024), pp. 618, 623.

138 Alles and Brun (2023), pp. 177, 185.

139 Hongler and Habich (2025), pp. 247–274.

140 Verbal statement First Session (6th Meeting) (n 44 in Chap. 2) 4; see also G20 Note (n 25 in Chap. 4) 28–35.

141 Written input Second Session (n 44 in Chap. 2) EU, Germany and Singapore.

142 Written inputs Second Session (n 44 in Chap. 2) Germany.

143 Written inputs Second Session (n 44 in Chap. 2) Singapore (see point 4).

144 Written inputs Second Session (n 44 in Chap. 2) US (see point 3).

145 United Nations (2015), para 22. Resolution 79/235 determines that 69/313 is one of a few resolutions recalled in the Preamble of the FTC, together with 70/1 of 2015 (Transforming Our World).

146 See below Sect. 7.4.

147 Occhiali et al. (2025); Bergolo et al. (2023), p. 530.

148 G20 Note (n 25 in Chap. 4); First Session (6th Meeting) (n 44 in Chap. 2).

reforms'.[149] The G20 Note continues, 'developing countries have an average tax gap of 9% of GDP, that is they raise less than what is possible, based on best-performing peers under similar circumstances'.[150] As the World Bank estimates the average LMIC tax revenue presently at below 10.5% of GDP, the potential for raising domestic tax revenue remains rather substantial.[151]

The significance of national tax systems to the pursuit of community interests, and potential state responsibility for the same, is confirmed and strengthened by the international courts' recent advisory opinions on climate change. These opinions consistently underscore that domestic implementation must be, 'concrete',[152] 'capable of making an adequate contribution',[153] not formulaic,[154] and 'function effectively'.[155] Similarly, International Tribunal for the Law of the Sea (ITLOS) posits that 'all necessary measures' to prevent, reduce and control pollution of the marine environment should be interpreted broadly,[156] and that States' duty of due diligence is an obligation to deploy adequate means, to exercise best possible efforts, to do the utmost,[157] to provide an 'effective response',[158] and to allocate "sufficient resources"[159] In that context, the opinions emphasise the means, capabilities and available resources of States,[160] while the Inter-American Court of Human Rights (IACtHR) explicitly refers to the tax capacity of States.[161] As recognized by the ICJ AO, the subsidization of fossil fuels—often in the form of tax exemptions—may trigger international liability, underscoring the critical role of taxation in climate mitigation measures. This article argues that, while they retain discretion, States' domestic climate measures -at least those requiring fiscal support- are not 'capable of making an adequate contribution'[162] if this support is not provided by the national

---

149 G20 Note (n 25 in Chap. 4) 4.

150 Ibid 4.

151 World Bank financial data <https://data.worldbank.org/indicator/GC.TAX.TOTL.GD.ZS?locations=XO> accessed 8 June 2025.

152 *Verein KlimaSeniorinnen and Others v Switzerland* App no 53600/20 (ECHR, 26 April 2022) (*KlimaSeniorinnen v Switzerland*), para 565.

153 International Court of Justice (ICJ) (2025), para 242.

154 International Court of Justice (ICJ) (2025), para 236.

155 International Court of Justice (ICJ) (2025), para 253. See also, on the principle of effectiveness in connection to procedural rights, EFTA Court, *The Norwegian State v Greenpeace Nordic, Nature and Youth Norway* (21 May 2025) Case E-18/24, paras 54–56 and 104.

156 UNCLOS (n 106 in this chapter) art 194(1); ITLOS *Climate Change Advisory Opinion* (n 34 in this chapter), para 203.

157 ITLOS *Climate Change Advisory Opinion* (n 34 in this chapter), para 233; see also ITLOS *Area Advisory Opinion* (n 36 in this chapter), para 110.

158 ITLOS *Climate Change Advisory Opinion* (n 34 in this chapter), para 212.

159 Ibid, para 241.

160 International Court of Justice (ICJ) (2025), para 291; ITLOS *Climate Change Advisory Opinion* (n 34 in this chapter), para 241.

161 *Climate Emergency and Human Rights*, Advisory Opinion AO-32/25, Inter-American Court of Human Rights (29 May 2025) (IACtHR AO), para 329.

162 International Court of Justice (ICJ) (2025), para 242.

tax system. As States are obligated to deploy 'all the measures at their disposal' or 'do the utmost' this refers not only to the tax system as presented, but this must encompass reforms if necessary to address deficiencies or insufficiencies, within States' national circumstances.

7.4 Human Rights

The invocation of respect for human rights as a core principle for the FTC was not determined from the outset of this UN effort. The reference to human rights was not expressly articulated in Resolution 78/230, yet it emerged as a recurrent theme during the First Session of the TOR Committee, particularly among civil society representatives.[163] Following its incorporation into the Zero Draft of the TOR, it provoked minimal debate within the Ad Hoc Committee. To the casual observer, linking respect for human rights to the FTC appears an indisputable necessity. The Universal Declaration of Human Rights is widely relied on by States, while the International Covenant on Civil and Political Rights (ICCPR) and the International Covenant on Economic, Social and Cultural Rights (ICESCR) have been extensively ratified.[164] The obligation to uphold human rights in the context of taxation is well-established. The legality of tax measures under human rights obligations may be examined through a broad spectrum of human rights protections, but primarily with regard to the protection of the right to property, as unlawful taxation may constitute an illicit deprivation of property, the protections against non-discrimination, and -in connection mainly with tax investigations and penalties- with the right to a fair trial and the right to a private home life.

Tax measures have only on relatively rare occasions been found to constitute a violation of the right to property, in large part due to the understanding that lawful taxes are necessary in the interest of the community, reflected in Prot. 1 Art. 1 para 2 reference to the securing the payment of taxes.[165] Violations of Article 1 of Protocol

[163] Centre for Economic and Social Rights, Inputs to the First Session (n 44 in Chap. 2); see also Tax Justice Network Africa, Written inputs Second Session (n 44 in Chap. 2).

[164] No reference is made in the requests to Convention on the Rights of the Child (adopted 20 November 1989, entered into force 2 September 1990) 1577 UNTS 3; International Convention on the Elimination of All Forms of Racial Discrimination (adopted 21 December 1965, entered into force 4 January 1969) 660 UNTS 195; Convention on the Elimination of All Forms of Discrimination against Women (adopted 18 December 1979, entered into force 3 September 1981) 1249 UNTS 1 (CEDAW); Convention on the Rights of Persons with Disabilities (signed 30 March 2007, entered into force 3 May 2008) 2515 UNTS 3; International Convention on the Protection of the Rights of All Migrant Workers and Members of their Families (signed 18 December 1990, entered into force 1 July 2003) 2220 UNTS 3 (ICRMW).

[165] The protection of property is included in the UDHR (n 12 in this chapter) article 17, but not in the ICCPR (n 11 in this chapter), or in the ICESCR (n 11 in this chapter). It is also mentioned in two UN Conventions, notably the CEDAW (n 164 in this chapter) art 16 and the ICRMW (n 164 in this chapter) art 15, and in UNGA Res 61/295 'United Nations Declaration on the Rights of

No. 1 were found in *S.A. Dangeville v. France*, *Intersplav v. Ukraine*, and *Bulves AD v. Bulgaria*,[166] where the deprivation of VAT reimbursements was deemed disproportionate and lacking sufficient public interest justification. Similarly, in *Buffalo Srl in liquidation v. Italy*, the European Court of Human Rights (ECtHR) ruled that delays by tax authorities in disbursing tax rebates caused disproportionate uncertainty and financial harm.[167] In *Di Belmonte v. Italy*, a violation was established due to the authorities' delay in executing a judgment, which resulted in the retroactive application of tax legislation imposing a 20% tax deduction at source on the applicant's expropriation compensation.[168] In *N.K.M. v. Hungary*, the applicant, a civil servant, contested a 98% tax imposed on part of her severance pay under legislation enacted shortly before her dismissal.[169] The ECtHR ruled in her favour, finding an unjustified deprivation of property.[170]

The FTC does not primarily emphasise the integration of human rights considerations within national tax systems. Rather, its focus lies in fostering international tax cooperation that aligns with states' obligations under international human rights law, as articulated in the directive to

> [b]e aligned, in the pursuit of international tax cooperation, with States' obligations under international human rights law.[171]

This orientation shifts the emphasis from domestic tax laws—where human rights typically intersect with taxation—to a broader international framework. Such alignment could manifest in various forms. For instance, states could enhance international cooperation under the FTC to ensure that national tax laws comply with international human rights standards, such as by collaboratively addressing and eliminating discriminatory tax practices at the national level.[172] However, in a

Indigenous Peoples' (2 October 2007) UN Doc A/RES/61/295 [United Nations General Assembly (UNGA), 2007]. The European Convention for the Protection of Human Rights and Fundamental Freedoms (adopted 4 November 1950, entered into force 3 September 1953) 213 UNTS 221 has included the right to property in art 1 of the First Protocol.

166 *S.A. Dangeville v. France* (Application No. 36677/97, ECtHR, 16 April 2002); *Intersplav v. Ukraine* (Application No. 803/02, ECtHR, 9 January 2007); *Bulves AD v. Bulgaria* (Application No. 3991/03, ECtHR, 22 January 2009).

167 *Buffalo Srl in liquidation v. Italy* (Application No. 38746/97, ECtHR, 3 July 2003).

168 *Di Belmonte v. Italy* (Application No. 72638/01, ECtHR, 16 March 2010).

169 *N.K.M. v. Hungary* (Application No. 66529/11, ECtHR, 14 May 2013).

170 *Pop and Others v Romania* no 39388/13 (ECHR, 30 June 2020); *Gasus Dosier- und Fördertechnik GmbH v Netherlands* no 15375/89 (ECHR, 23 February 1995); *National and Provincial Building Society, Leeds Permanent Building Society and Yorkshire Building Society v United Kingdom* no 21319/93, 21449/93, and 21675/93 (ECHR, 23 October 1997); *Imbert de Trémiolles v France* no 25834/94 (ECHR, 4 April 1996); *Eko-Elda AVEE v Greece* no 10162/02 (ECHR, 21 March 2006); *Cacciato v Italy* no 60903/00 (ECHR, 16 November 2006) and *Guiso and Consiglio v Italy* no 5089/03 (ECHR, 21 March 2006).

171 United Nations General Assembly (UNGA) (2024), para 9(c).

172 CESCR (2015), para 11; Committee on the Elimination of Discrimination against Women (CEDAW) (2008), paras 32–33; Committee on the Elimination of Racial Discrimination (CERD) (2017), paras 23–24.

broader context, international cooperation aligned with human rights obligations may necessitate that states facilitate the mobilisation of tax resources to fulfil their human rights commitments. Both approaches are discussed in turn.

7.4.1 International Cooperation to Address Individual Tax Measures Contravening Human Rights Norms

Cooperation between FTC parties may be aimed at ensuring that individual national tax measures do not breach human rights norms, in a coordinated approach. The human rights protections most likely to be involved in such an effort can be gleaned from the case law of the international human rights courts and UN human rights treaty body outputs.

Discriminatory taxes were alleged in *J.D. and A v. the United Kingdom*, where an applicant submitted that rules on housing benefit in the social housing sector (informally known as "the bedroom tax") discriminated against her because of her particular situation as a victim of gender based violence, which required her to have "panic room" installed in the attic.[173] The Court held that there had been a violation of Article 14 (prohibition of discrimination) of the Convention in conjunction with Article 1 (protection of property) of Protocol No. 1 in respect of the second applicant. In *Glor v. Switzerland*, the applicant, deemed unfit for military service due to diabetes, was nonetheless required to pay a tax for exemption from such service,[174] which the ECtHR found to constitute a violation of Article 14 (prohibition of discrimination) in conjunction with Article 8 (right to respect for private and family life). The ECtHR did not agree, however, that differentiation in tax imposts between married and unmarried cohabitants constituted discrimination in *Burden v. United Kingdom*, a claim lodged by two elderly unmarried sisters.[175]

Although the ECtHR's protection of the right to a fair trial does not apply to disputes between citizens and public authorities regarding the lawfulness of tax decisions,[176] taxpayers frequently challenge certain other aspects of tax proceedings, as illustrated by *Jussila v. Finland*, where the applicant alleged a violation of this right due to tax surcharges.[177] The European Court of Human Rights (ECtHR) held that the proceedings were not criminal in nature, thus warranting a lower degree of procedural protections. Similarly, in *Melgarejo Martinez de Abellanosa v.*

---

[173] *J.D. and A v. the United Kingdom* (Application Nos. 32949/17 and 34614/17, ECtHR, 24 October 2019).

[174] *Glor v. Switzerland* (Application No. 13444/04, ECtHR, 30 April 2009).

[175] *Burden v. United Kingdom* (Application No. 13378/05, ECtHR, 29 April 2008).

[176] *Ferrazzini v Italy* no 44759/98 (ECHR, 12 July 2001).

[177] *Jussila v. Finland* (Application No. 73053/01, ECtHR, 23 November 2006).

Spain, fair trial concerns were raised.[178] In *Vegotex International S.A. v. Belgium*, the ECtHR found a violation due to the excessive length of tax recovery proceedings (exceeding 13 years).[179] In *J.J. v. Netherlands* (Application No. 21351/93, ECtHR, 27 March 1998), the applicant, a tax consultant, argued that his right to a fair trial was violated because he was unable to respond to an advisory opinion submitted by the Advocate-General to the Supreme Court in proceedings determining a criminal charge against him.[180] The ECtHR ruled in his favour, finding a violation of Article 6 § 1.

The right to privacy has on occasion been invoked in connection with home searches in the context of tax investigations, such as in *Brazzi v. Italy*,[181] or concerning the release of information, as in *L.B. v. Hungary*,[182] concerning the publication of a tax offenders' list, regarding a warrantless home search.[183] In *Melo Tadeu v. Portugal*, the applicant argued that tax enforcement measures and asset attachment persisted despite her acquittal in criminal proceedings for tax fraud.[184] The ECtHR held that there was a violation of Article 6 § 2 (presumption of innocence) and Article 1 of Protocol No. 1 (protection of property), concluding that the authorities' disregard for her acquittal and failure to maintain a fair balance constituted breaches of her rights.[185]

Other rights that have been invoked in tax cases include religious freedom,[186] the right not to be tried or punished twice,[187] the presumption of innocence[188] and the freedom of movement.[189]

---

178 *Melgarejo Martinez de Abellanosa v. Spain* (Application No. 11200/19, ECtHR, 14 December 2021).

179 *Vegotex International S.A. v. Belgium* (Application No. 49812/09, ECtHR, 3 November 2022).

180 *J.J. v. Netherlands* (Application No. 21351/93, ECtHR, 27 March 1998).

181 *Brazzi v. Italy* (Application No. 57278/11, ECtHR, 27 September 2018).

182 *L.B. v. Hungary* (Application No. 36345/16, ECtHR, 9 March 2023).

183 *Keslassy v France* no 64104/00 (ECHR, 29 April 2003); see however *Bernh Larsen Holding AS and Others v Norway* no 24117/08 (ECHR, 14 March 2013).

184 *Melo Tadeu v. Portugal* (Application No. 27785/09, ECtHR, 23 October 2014).

185 *Bendenoun v France* no 12547/86 (ECHR, 24 February 1994); *J.B. v Switzerland* no 31827/96 (ECHR, 3 May 2001); *K.S. and M.S. v Germany* no 33696/11 (ECHR, 6 October 2016); *André and Others v France* no 18603/03 (ECHR, 24 July 2008).

186 *Association Les Témoins de Jéhovah v France* no 8916/05 (ECHR, 30 June 2011); *Klein and Others v Germany* no 10138/11 (ECHR, 13 November 2017); *The Church of Jesus Christ of Latter-Day Saints v the United Kingdom* no 7552/09 (ECHR, 4 March 2014); *Assemblée Chrétienne Des Témoins de Jéhovah d'Anderlecht and Others v Belgium* no 20165/20 (ECHR, 5 April 2022).

187 *Ruotsalainen v Finland* no 13079/03 (ECHR, 16 June 2009); *Johannesson and Others v Iceland* no 22007/11 (ECHR, 18 May 2017); *Lucky Dev v Sweden* no 7356/10 (ECHR, 27 November 2014); *A. and B. v Norway* no 24130/11 and 29758/11 (ECHR, 15 November 2016).

188 In *A.P., M.P. and T.P. v Switzerland* no 19958/92 (ECHR, 29 August 1997); *Janosevic v Sweden* no 34619/97 (ECHR, 23 July 2002) and *Västberga Taxi Aktiebolag and Vulic v Sweden* no 36985/97 (ECHR, 23 July 2002); *Melo Tadeu v Portugal* no 27785/09 (ECHR, 23 October 2014).

189 *Société Oxygène Plus v France* no 76935/11 (ECHR, 17 May 2016).

The findings of UN human rights treaty bodies identify various infringements of human rights protections by national tax measures of states, particularly in connection with gender and racial discrimination and the rights children. For example, the Committee on the Elimination of Discrimination against Women (CEDAW) expressed concern over the disproportionately high poverty rates among women in the Bahamas the Committee recommended that the Bahamas align its financial and tax policies to avoid negative impacts on women's rights and to advance substantive equality between women and men.[190] CEDAW also highlighted discriminatory tax practices in Lebanon, noting that married women are treated as single for taxation purposes, thereby being denied the same tax allowances granted to married men or heads of household. The Committee called on Lebanon to implement measures to eliminate this form of discrimination in its taxation framework.[191] The Committee on the Elimination of Racial Discrimination (CERD) raised concerns regarding Belarus' so-called 'social parasitism' tax, instituted under Presidential Decree No. 3 (2015), which mandated that individuals working fewer than 183 days annually pay approximately $250 per year to compensate for lost tax revenue. The Committee noted that this tax disproportionately impacted the Roma community. Although the tax was suspended in 2017 and a revised draft was under consideration, CERD urged Belarus to refrain from implementing taxes that disproportionately affect disadvantaged ethnic minorities, specifically highlighting taxes predicated on unemployment or underemployment, such as the 'social parasitism' tax.[192]

7.4.2 The General Adequacy of National Tax Systems to Ensure the Capacity to Finance Human Rights Objectives

In a broader sense, international cooperation aligned with human rights may focus on the general design and administration of the tax system, in both its national and international dimensions. A recent statement by the Committee for the CESCR suggests for the national aspects that:

> States Parties could consider taking measures such as: (a) ensuring that those with higher income and wealth, in particular those at the top of the income and wealth spectrums, are subject to a proportionate and appropriate tax burden; (b) shifting focus to a more direct income taxation approach rather than relying on indirect taxes, such as value added tax and goods and services tax, which tend to disproportionately affect individuals and families with lower incomes; and (c) levying adequate taxation on the profits of large companies, in

[190] CEDAW, 'Concluding observations on the sixth periodic report of the Bahamas' (14 November 2018) UN Doc CEDAW/C/BHS/CO/6, paras 39–40.

[191] CEDAW (n 164 in this chapter), paras 32–33.

[192] CERD (n 164 in this chapter), paras 23–24.

particular multinational companies domiciled or operating in the State Party and on high-net-worth individuals[193]

UN human rights treaty bodies have regularly addressed the design and efficiency of national tax systems. For example, in its Concluding Observations, the Committee on Economic, Social and Cultural Rights (CESCR) expressed concern that IFFs from third countries continue to be channelled through financial institutions in Switzerland. The Committee noted that such practices reduce the availability of financial resources essential for realising economic, social, and cultural rights in the affected countries. It urged Switzerland to implement stringent measures to combat tax evasion, particularly by corporations and high-net-worth individuals, and to strengthen efforts to address global tax abuse. This includes ensuring robust regulation of financial institutions to prevent fraud and tax evasion schemes.[194] The CESCR also raised concerns about the low corporate income tax rate in Mauritius, cautioning that it could diminish public revenues necessary for implementing Covenant rights. The Committee further warned that such a low rate might encourage 'unhealthy regulatory competition' within the subregion, impeding regional governments' ability to mobilise resources critical for fulfilling human rights obligations. The CESCR recommended that Mauritius reassess the role of corporate income tax in generating domestic revenue and actively pursue upward harmonisation of corporate taxation in the region to enhance foreign investors' contributions to public funds.[195] In other Concluding Observations, the Committee has suggested the need for reforming the national tax system to improve the general ability to collect taxes,[196] enhance progressivity,[197] to tax emissions,[198] include more groups of

[193] CESCR Statement (n 89 in this chapter), para 6.

[194] CESCR, 'Concluding observations on the fourth periodic report of Switzerland' (18 November 2019) UN Doc E/C.12/CHE/CO/44, paras 12–13.

[195] CESCR, 'Concluding observations on the fifth periodic report of Mauritius' (5 April 2019) UN Doc E/C.12/MUS/CO/5, paras 13–14.

[196] CESCR, 'Concluding observations on the initial report of the State of Palestine' (1 November 2023) UN Doc E/C.12/PSE/CO/1, para 18.

[197] CESCR, 'Concluding observations on the seventh periodic report of the Philippines' (25 March 2025) UN Doc E/C.12/PHL/CO/7, para 17(d); see also United Nations Committee on the Rights of the Child, 'Consideration of reports submitted by States Parties under article 44 of the Convention: Concluding observations: Guatemala' (25 October 2010) UN Doc CRC/C/GTM/CO/3–4. On progressivity, see also CESCR Statement (n 89 in this chapter), para 4; United Nations Human Rights Council, 'Report of the Special Rapporteur on extreme poverty and human rights, Philip Alston' (27 May 2015) UN Doc A/HRC/29/31, para 53; UNGA, 'The role of the United Nations in promoting a new global human order and an assessment of the implications of inequality for development: Report of the Secretary-General' (26 September 2012) UN Doc A/67/394.

[198] CESCR, 'Concluding observations on the third periodic report of China, including Hong Kong, China, and Macao, China' (22 March 2023) UN Doc E/C.12/CHN/CO/3, para 25(a); CESCR, 'Concluding observations on the fourth periodic report of Ireland' (20 March 2024) UN Doc E/C.12/IRL/CO/4, para 13(a); CESCR, 'Concluding observations on the sixth periodic report of Italy' (7 December 2022) UN Doc E/C.12/ITA/CO/6, para 18(a); CESCR, 'Concluding observations on the seventh periodic report of Poland' (24 October 2024) UN Doc E/C.12/POL/CO/7, para 17(a).

taxpayers in the tax base,[199] adopt anti-avoidance measures,[200] and increase taxes on tobacco or alcohol.[201]

The linkage between domestic tax policies and human rights is underscored by the IACtHR in its Advisory Opinion on the Climate Emergency and Human Rights, particularly as a potential subject matter for international cooperation. The IACtHR observes that deficiencies or limitations in tax systems lead to insufficient funding for climate-related human rights protections.[202] In this context, the IACtHR highlights the importance of design options, the extent of progressivity, and international coordination in addressing tax evasion, stating:

> The Court also notes that, in fulfilling the obligation of cooperation, States can promote coordinated measures on matters such as progressive taxation, strengthening tax collection capacities, and combatting tax evasion, corruption, and illicit financial flows.[203]

In *Klimaseniorinnen* the planned Swiss carbon tax, which was postponed and watered down several times, was one of the facts the ECtHR took into account in its ultimate decision against the Swiss Government for having violated human rights with its inadequate climate actions[204] Assessments by adjudicatory bodies on the general tax policy or specific tax measures by states are fettered by the entrenched position that States should be afforded additional deference and discretion in the exercise of their fiscal policies.[205]

However, it is crucial to emphasize that, even if the reallocation of taxing rights to a particular state or a coalition of states is somehow executed, there is no inherent assurance that the resulting tax revenues will be directed toward financing initiatives that promote human rights. This highlights a profound and enduring disparity between the generation of tax revenue and the effective implementation of policies designed to achieve substantive, long-term environmental, social, and economic outcomes.[206]

---

[199] CESCR, 'Concluding observations on the fifth periodic report of Iraq' (14 March 2024) UN Doc E/C.12/IRQ/CO/5, para 17.

[200] CESCR, 'Concluding observations on the fourth periodic report of Ireland' (20 March 2024) UN Doc E/C.12/IRL/CO/4, para 15(d).

[201] CESCR, 'Concluding observations on the sixth periodic report of Italy' (7 December 2022) UN Doc E/C.12/ITA/CO/6, para 56.

[202] International Monetary Fund, *IMF Fiscal Monitor: Tackling Inequality* (2017) 10; 'Draft resolution submitted by the President of the Conference: Sevilla Commitment' UN Fourth International Conference on Financing for Development (Sevilla, 30 June-3 July 2025) (18 June 2025) UN Doc A/CONF.227/2025/L.1, para 26; Report of the United Nations High Commissioner for Human Rights (14 April 2022) UN Doc A/HRC/50/51, para 80; IACtHR AO (n 161 in this chapter), para 263.

[203] IACtHR AO (n 161 in this chapter), para 263.

[204] *KlimaSeniorinnen v Switzerland* (n 152 in this chapter), paras 86, 93, 96, 97, 124.

[205] *Christian Religious Organization of Jehovah's Witnesses in the NKR v Armenia* no 41817/10 (ECHR, 22 March 2022), para 50; *Bežanić and Baškarad v Croatia* no 16140/15 and 13322/16 (ECHR, 19 May 2022), para 64.

[206] Stark (2022).

Case Law

André and Others v France, No. 18603/03 (ECHR July 24, 2008).
Application of the Convention on the Prevention and Punishment of the Crime of Genocide (The Gambia v Myanmar: 7 States Intervening), 477 ICJ Reports (2022).
Arbitration Regarding the Iron Rhine ("Ijzeren Rijn") Railway between the Kingdom of Belgium and the Kingdom of the Netherlands, XXVII Reports of International Arbitral Awards (RIAA) para 59 (PCA 2005).
Bendenoun v France, No. 12547/86 (ECHR February 24, 1994).
Bernh Larsen Holding AS and Others v Norway, No. 24117/08 (ECHR March 14, 2013).
Buffalo Srl in Liquidation v. Italy, No. 38746/97 (ICJ July 3, 2003).
Burden v. United Kingdom, No. 13378/05 (ICJ April 29, 2008).
Cacciato v Italy, No. 60903/00 (ECHR November 16, 2006).
Climate Emergency and Human Rights (IACtHR May 29, 2025).
Continental Shelf (Tunisia/Libyan Arab Jamahiriya), 18 ICJ Rep para 71 (1982).
Corfu Channel (UK v Albania), ICJ Reports 4 (1949).
Di Belmonte v. Italy, No. 72638/01 (ICJ March 16, 2010).
Dispute over the Status and Use of the Waters of the Silala (Chile v Bolivia), 614 ICJ Reports paras 83 and 99 (2022).
Eko-Elda AVEE v Greece, No. 10162/02 (ECHR March 21, 2006).
European Commission v European Food SA and Others, No. C-638/19 (2022).
European Commission v United Kingdom of Great Britain and Northern Ireland, No. C-516/22 (2024).
European Food SA and Others v European Commission, No. T-624/15, T-694/15, T-704/15 (2019).
Factory Chorzów (Germany v Poland), Series A No 17 PCIJ 29 (PCIJ 1928).
Ferrazzini v Italy, No. 44759/98 (ECHR July 12, 2001).
Gabčíkovo-Nagymaros Separate Opinion of Vice-President Weeramantry, 88 ICJ Reports (1997).
Gasus Dosier- Und Fördertechnik GmbH v Netherlands, No. 15375/89 (ECHR February 23, 1995).
Glor v. Switzerland, No. 13444/04 (International Court of Justice (ICJ) April 30, 2009).
Guiso and Consiglio v Italy, No. 5089/03 (European Convention on Human Rights (ECHR) March 21, 2006).
Imbert de Trémiolles v France, No. 25834/94 (European Convention on Human Rights (ECHR) April 4, 1996).
Intersplav v. Ukraine, No. 803/02 (ICJ January 9, 2007).
J.B. v Switzerland, No. 31827/96 (ECHR May 3, 2001).
J.D. and A v. the United Kingdom, No. 32949/17, 34614/17 (ICJ October 24, 2019).
J.J. v. Netherlands, No. 21351/93 (ICJ March 27, 1998).
Jussila v. Finland, No. 73053/01 (ICJ November 23, 2006).
Keslassy v France, No. 64104/00 (ECHR April 29, 2003).

K.S. and M.S. v Germany, No. 33696/11 (ECHR October 6, 2016).
Legality of the Threat or Use of Nuclear Weapons, 226 ICJ Rep para 27 (1996).
Loan Agreement between Italy and Costa Rica (Dispute Arising under a Financing Agreement), 25 RIAA 23 (PCA 1998).
Melgarejo Martinez de Abellanosa v. Spain, No. 11200/19 (ICJ December 14, 2021).
National and Provincial Building Society, Leeds Permanent Building Society and Yorkshire Building Society v United Kingdom, No. 21319/93, 21449/93, and 21675/93 (ECHR October 23, 1997).
N.K.M. v. Hungary, No. 66529/11 (ICJ May 14, 2013).
North Sea Continental Shelf (Germany v Netherlands/Denmark), 3 ICJ Rep para 74 (1969).
Nuclear Tests (Australia v. France), 253, 268 ICJ Reports (1974).
Pop and Others v Romania, No. 39388/13 (ECHR June 30, 2020).
Pulp Mills on the River Uruguay (Argentina v Uruguay), 14 ICJ Reports para 101 (ICJ 2010).
Request for an Advisory Opinion Submitted by the Commission of Small Island States on Climate Change and International Law, Case No. 31 ITLOS para 235 (2024). https://www.itlos.org/fileadmin/itlos/documents/cases/31/Advisory_Opinion/C31_Adv_Op_21.05.2024_corr.pdf
Reservations to the Convention on Genocide, ICJ Reports 23 (1951). (Gambia v Myanmar)
Responsibilities and Obligations of States Sponsoring Persons and Entities with Respect to Activities in the Area, Case No. 17 ITLOS para 131 (2011).
S.A. Dangeville v. France, No. 36677/97 (ICJ April 16, 2002).
Temple of Preah Vihear (Cambodia v. Thailand), 6 ICJ Reports (1962).
The Norwegian State v Greenpeace Nordic, Nature and Youth Norway (EFTA Court May 21, 2025).
Trail Smelter Arbitration (UNRIAA April 16, 1938).
Vegotex International S.A. v. Belgium, No. 49812/09 (ICJ November 3, 2022).
Verein KlimaSeniorinnen and Others v Switzerland (April 26, 2022).

References

Alles, D., & Brun, E. (2023). Mobilizing the south: Pluralizing and complexifying multilateralism. In G. Aurianne (Ed.), *Crisis of multilateralism? Challenges and resilience* (pp. 177, 185). Springer/Palgrave.

Atapattu, S. (2019). From our common future to sustainable development goals: Evolution of sustainable development under international law. *Wisconsin International Law Journal*, *36*(2), 215, 237.

Avi-Yonah, R. S. (2016). Hanging together: A multilateral approach to taxing multinationals. *Michigan Business & Entrepreneurial Law Review*, *5*(2), 137.

Barral, V. (2012). Sustainable development in international law: Nature and operation of an evolutive legal norm. *European Journal of International Law*, *23*, 377–400.

Benvenisti, E., & Nolte, G. (2018). Introduction. In E. Benvenisti & G. Nolte (Eds.), *Community interests across international law* (p. 5). OUP.

Bergolo, M., Londoño-Vélez, J., & Tortarolo, D. (2023). Tax progressivity and taxing the rich in developing countries: Lessons from Latin America. *Oxford Review of Economic Policy, 39*(3), 530.

Besson, S. (2018). In E. Benvenisti, G. Nolte, & K. Yalin-Mor (Eds.), *Community interests in international law: Whose interests are they and how should we best identify them?* Oxford University Press.

Beyerlin, U., & Marauhn, T. (2011). *International environmental law*. Hart/Beck.

Birnie, P. W., Boyle, A. E., & Redgwell, C. (2009). *International law and the environment* (3rd ed.). Oxford University Press.

Black, S., Parry, I. W. H., Singh, S., & Vernon-Lin, N. (2024). *Destination net zero: The urgent need for a global carbon tax on aviation and shipping* (No. 2024/003; IMF Staff Climate Note, p. 11). International Monetary Fund.

Boyle, A., & Freestone, D. (Eds.). (1999). *International law and sustainable development*. Oxford University Press.

Brock, G., & Pogge, T. (2014). Global tax justice and global justice. In *Moral philosophy and politics* (Vol. 1, p. 1).

Brooks, K., & Krever, R. (2015). The troubling role of tax treaties. In G. M. M. Michielse & V. Thuronyi (Eds.), *Tax design issues worldwide* (pp. 159, 166). Wolters Kluwer Law & Business.

Brownlie, I. (1998). *Principles of public international law* (3rd ed.). Oxford University Press.

Brundtland, G. H. (1987). *Our common future: The World Commission on Environment and Development*. Oxford University Press.

Burgers, I. J. J., & Mosquera Valderrama, I. J. (2017). Fairness: A dire international tax standard with no meaning? *Intertax, 45*(12), 767.

CEDAW. (2008). *Concluding comments of the Committee on the Elimination of Discrimination against Women: Lebanon* (No. UN Doc CEDAW/C/LBN/CO/3; p. para 32–33).

CERD. (2017). *Concluding observations on the combined twentieth to twenty-third periodic reports of Belarus* (No. UN Doc CERD/C/BLR/CO/20-23; p. paras 23–24).

CESCR. (2015). *Concluding observations on the third periodic report of Ireland* (No. UN Doc E/C.12/IRL/CO/3; p. para 11).

CESCR. (2021). *Statement on tax policy and the International Covenant on Economic, Social and Cultural Rights* (No. E/C.12/2025/1). Retrieved September 5, 2025, from https://www.cesr.org/sites/default/files/2025/Statement_on_Tax_Policy_and_the_International_Covenant_on_Economic_Social_and_Cultural_Rights.pdf

Christensen, R. C., Hearson, M., & Randriamanalina, T. (2020). *At the table, off the menu: Assessing the participation of lower-income countries in global tax negotiations* (No. Working Paper 115). International Centre of Tax and Development, Institute of Development Studies. https://www.ictd.ac/publication/table-off-menu-participation-lower-income-countries-tax-negotiations

Dagan, T. (2017). International tax and global justice. *Theoretical Inquiries in Law, 18*, 34.

Dagan, T. (2018). Community interests in international taxation. In E. Benvenisti & G. Nolte (Eds.), *Community interests across international law* (p. 336). OUP.

Devereux, M., & Vella, J. (2014). Are we heading towards a corporate tax system fit for the 21st century? *Fiscal Studies & Intertax, 35*(4), 449.

European Commission. (2015). *Investment in TTIP and beyond – The path for reform. Enhancing the right to regulate and moving from current ad hoc arbitration towards an Investment Court* (p. 5) [Concept paper]. Retrieved June 2, 2025, from https://ec.europa.eu/commission/presscorner/detail/en/ip_15_5651

European Union (EU). (2003). *Restructuring the Community Framework for the Taxation of Energy Products and Electricity* (No. OJ L283/51; p. Article 14(1)(b) and (c)). Official Journal of the European Union.

European Union (EU). (2013). *Arbitral award Micula v Romania of 11 December 2013* (No. SA.38517 (2014/C) (ex 2014/NN)).

European Union (EU). (2021). *Proposal for a Council Directive restructuring the Union Framework for the Taxation of Energy Products and Electricity* (EU Legislative Proposal No. COM (2021); p. 563 final).

Faber, J., Leestemaker, L., & van den Berg, R. (2022). Maritime shipping and EU ETS: An assessment of the possibilities to evade ETS costs. *CE Delft*. Retrieved November 25, 2025, from https://cedelft.eu/publications/maritime-shipping-and-eu-ets-an-assessment-of-the-possibilities-to-evade-ets-costs/

Faccio, T., & Ghosh, J. (2024). Why should EU countries support a UN Framework Convention on International Tax Cooperation. *Intertax, 52*(5), 358.

Feichtner, I. (2012). Community interests. *Max Planck Encyclopedia of Public International Law*, para 2.

Franck, T. M. (1998). *Fairness in international law and institutions* (pp. 2–24). Oxford University Press.

French, D. (2005). *International law and policy of sustainable development*. Manchester University Press.

Global Solidarity Levies Task Force. (n.d.). *About*. Retrieved October 16, 2024, from https://globalsolidaritylevies.org/about/

Graetz, M. J. (1991). Taxing international income: Inadequate principles, outdated concepts and unsatisfactory policies. *54*, 261, 262.

Gribnau, H., & Jallai, A.-G. (2018). *Sustainable tax governance and transparency* (Tilburg Law School Research Paper). Retrieved June 8, 2025, from https://ssrn.com/abstract=3273553 or http://dx.doi.org/10.2139/ssrn.3273553

Group of Twenty (G20). (2023). *G20 New Delhi Leaders' Declaration* (p. para 62). Retrieved June 8, 2025, from https://www.g20.in/en/media-resources/documents/doc-outcomes.html

Henry, J. S. (2016). Let's tax anonymous wealth! A modest proposal to reduce inequality, attack organized crime, aid developing countries, and raise badly needed revenue from the world's wealthiest tax dodgers, Kleptocrats and Felons. In T. Pogge & K. Mehta (Eds.), *Global tax fairness* (p. 43). Oxford University Press.

Higgins, R. (1995). *Problems and process: International law and how we use it*. Oxford University Press.

Higgins, R. (1999). International law in a changing international system. *Cambridge Law Journal, 58*(1), 78, 84–85.

Hongler, P. (2021). *The international law of taxation*. Oxford University Press.

Hongler, P., & Habich, S. (2025). Plurilateralism in international tax law a unique chance for the UN Framework Tax Convention. *Journal of World Investment and Trade, 26*, 247–274.

International Bar Association. (2013). *Tax abuses, poverty and human rights*.

International Civil Aviation Organization (ICAO). (1993). *Council Resolution of 14 December 1993 on Taxation of Fuel, Lubricants and other Consumable Technical Supplies*. ICAO.

International Civil Aviation Organization (ICAO). (2016). *Consolidated statement of continuing ICAO policies and practices related to environmental protection – Global Market-based Measure (MBM) Scheme* (Assembly Resolution Nos. A39-3). ICAO.

International Court of Justice (ICJ). (2025, July 23). *Obligations of States in respect of climate change (ICJ AO)*. Retrieved July 27, 2025, from https://www.icj-cij.org/sites/default/files/case-related/187/187-20250723-adv-01-00-en.pdf

Jennings, R. Y. (1986). Equity and equitable principles. *Annuaire Suisse de Droit International, 42*(27), 35.

Keller, M. (Ed.). (2023). Article 8.9 Investment and regulatory measures. In *EU investment protection law: Article-by-article commentary* (Vol. 159, p. para 40). Beck/Hart.

Lydgate, E. B. (2012). Sustainable development in the WTO: From mutual supportiveness to balancing. *World Trade Review, 11*(4), 621, 626.

Meyer-Nandi, S. (2021). Policy coherence for sustainable development in international tax matters: A way forward for donor countries? In I. J. M. Valderrama, D. Lesage, & W. Lips (Eds.),

Taxation, international cooperation and the 2030 sustainable development agenda (pp. 63–64). Springer.
Occhiali, G., Mascagni, G., Prichard, W., & Hearson, M. (2025). *Taxing the wealthy in lower-income countries: Why it's important, and how to do it* (No. Policy Brief; p. 14). ICTD. Retrieved June 8, 2025, from https://www.ictd.ac/publication/taxing-wealthy-lower-income-countries-why-how/
OECD. (2009). *Engaging with high net worth individuals on tax compliance*. Organisation for Economic Cooperation and Development.
OECD. (2017). *UN Model Tax Convention on Income and on Capital: Condensed Version 2017*. Organisation for Economic Cooperation and Development.
OECD. (2021). *Developing countries and the OECD/G20 inclusive framework on BEPS: OECD report for the G20 Finance Ministers and Central Bank Governors* (pp. 18, 25). Organisation for Economic Cooperation and Development.
OECD. (2023). *138 countries and jurisdiction agree historic milestone to implement global tax deal*. OECD Press release. Retrieved June 10, 2025, from https://www.oecd.org/en/about/news/press-releases/2023/07/138-countries-and-jurisdictions-agree-historic-milestone-to-implement-global-tax-deal.html
Ozai, I. (2020). Two accounts of International Tax Justice. *Canadian Journal of Law & Jurisprudence, 33*(2), 317, 324.
Ozai, I. (2025). Global justice in the reshaping of international tax. *JIEL, 27*, 639, 642.
Parada, L. (2025). Global minimum taxation: A strategic approach for developing countries. *Columbia Journal of Tax Law, 15*(52), 188, 210.
Parry, I. W. H., Heine, D., Kizzier, K., & Smith, T. (2018). *Carbon taxation for international maritime fuels: Assessing the options* (No. WP/18/203; IMF Working Paper, p. 5). International Monetary Fund.
Persson, Å., Weitz, N., & Nilsson, M. (2016). Follow-up and review of the sustainable development goals: Alignment vs. Internalization. *Review of European, Comparative & International Environmental Law (RECIEL), 25*(1), 59, 63.
Pigou, A. C. (1920). *The economics of welfare*.
Pirlot, A. (2020a). A legal analysis of the mutual interactions between the UN sustainable development goals (SDGs) & taxation. In C. Brokelind & S. van Thiel (Eds.), *Tax sustainability in the EU and international context*. IBFD.
Pirlot, A. (2020b). The vagueness of tax fairness. A discursive analysis of the Commission's fair tax agenda. *Intertax, 48*(4), 402.
Pogge, T., & Mehtha, K. (2016). Introduction. In T. Pogge & K. Mehtha (Eds.), *Global tax fairness* (p. 43). OUP.
Ramlogan, R. (2011). *Sustainable development: Towards a judicial interpretation*. Nijhoff.
Rosenne, S. (1988). The position of the International Court of Justice on the foundation of the principle of equity in international law. *Europa Institut, 85*, 88–89.
Sands, P. (1999). International courts and the application of the concept of "sustainable development." *Max Planck Yearbook of United Nations Law Online, 3*(1), 389, 399.
Sands, P., Peel, J., Fabra, A., & MacKenzie, R. (2012). *Principles of international environmental law* (3rd ed., p. 206). Cambridge University Press (CUP).
Schill, S., & Djanic, V. (2018). International investment law and community interests. In E. Benvenisti & G. Nolte (Eds.), *Community interests across international law*. OUP.
Schrijver, N. (2008). *The evolution of sustainable development in international law: Inception, meaning and status*. Hague Academy of International Law.
Simma, B. (1994). *From bilateralism to community interest in international law* (Vol. 250, p. 233). Hague Academy of International Law.
Sorace, F. (2024, November 14). Yet another chapter in the Micula Saga: The EU General Court confirms the qualification of the Micula Award as state aid. *Kluwer Arbitration Blog*. Retrieved June 2, 2025, from https://arbitrationblog.kluwerarbitration.com/2024/11/14/yet-another-chapter-in-the-micula-saga-the-eu-general-court-confirms-the-qualification-of-the-micula-award-as-state-aid/

Stark, J. (2022). Tax justice beyond national borders—International or interpersonal? *Oxford Journal of Legal Studies, 42*(1), 133.

Stewart, M. (2024). International institutions in global tax governance. *Journal of International Economic Law, 27*(4), 618, 623.

Thin, S. (2021). Community interest and the international public legal order. *Netherlands International Law Review (NILR), 68*(35), 55.

Tietje, C., & Lang, A. (2018). Community interests in world trade law. In E. Benvenisti & G. Nolte (Eds.), *Community interests across international law* (p. 192). OUP.

UN World Commission on Environment and Development. (1987). *Our common future* (No. UN Doc A/42/427; p. 43).

United Nations. (1972). *Declaration of the United Nations Conference on the Human Environment* (No. UN Doc A/CONF.48/14/Rev.1; p. Principle 21).

United Nations. (1992). *Rio Declaration on Environment and Development* (No. UN Doc A/CONF.151/26). UN Conference on Environment and Development.

United Nations. (2003). *United Nations Convention against Corruption* (No. UN Doc A/RES/58/4; p. art 62 (1)).

United Nations. (2015). *Resolution 69/313: Addis Ababa Action Agenda of the Third International Conference on Financing for Development* (No. UN Doc A/RES/69/313). United Nations. https://www.un.org/esa/ffd/wp-content/uploads/2015/08/AAAA_Outcome.pdf

Inputs to the First Session: United Nations Ad Hoc Committee to Draft Terms of Reference for a United Nations Framework Convention on International Tax Cooperation. https://financing.desa.un.org/un-tax-convention/first-session

Inputs to the Second Session: United Nations Committee to Draft Terms of Reference for a United Nations Framework Convention on International Tax Cooperation. https://financing.desa.un.org/un-tax-convention/second-session

United Nations General Assembly (UNGA). (1948). *Preamble of the Universal Declaration of Human Rights* (Treaty No. UNGA Res 217 (III)).

United Nations General Assembly (UNGA). (1974a). *Charter of Economic Rights and Duties of States* (No. UNGA Res 3281 (XXIX)).

United Nations General Assembly (UNGA). (1974b). *Declaration on the establishment of a new international economic order* (No. Res 3201 (S-VI)).

United Nations General Assembly (UNGA). (2005). *2005 World Summit Outcome* (No. UNGA Res 60/1; p. para 48).

United Nations General Assembly (UNGA). (2007). *Declaration on the Rights of Indigenous People* (No. UN Doc A/RES/61/295).

United Nations General Assembly (UNGA). (2015). *Resolution 70/1: Transforming our world: The 2030 agenda for sustainable development* (No. UN Doc A/RES/70/1). United Nations General Assembly.

United Nations General Assembly (UNGA). (2023a). *Promotion of inclusive and effective international tax cooperation at the United Nations: Report of the Secretary-General 78/235 (SG Report)* (No. UN Doc A/78/235).

United Nations General Assembly (UNGA). (2023b). *Resolution 78/230: Promotion of inclusive and effective International Tax Cooperation at the United Nations* (No. UN Doc A/RES/78/230). United Nations General Assembly.

United Nations General Assembly (UNGA). (2024). *Chair's proposal for draft terms of reference (TOR)* (No. UN Doc A/AC.295/2024/L.4.).

United Nations General Assembly (UNGA) Human Rights Council. (2025). *Understanding the landscape of climate finance, debt, tax and illicit financial flows and human rights* (No. UN Doc A/HRC/58/51).

van Hees, S. R. W. (2014). Sustainable development in the EU: Redefining and operationalizing the concept. *Utrecht Law Review*, 60.

Vanderbruggen, E. (2002). Tax treaty renegotiations by developing countries: A case study using comparative analysis to access the feasibility of achieving policy objectives. *Asia-Pacific Tax Bulletin, 8*(7/8).

Vogel, K. (1988). Worldwide vs. Source taxation of income – A review and re-evaluation of arguments (Part I). *Intertax, 16*(8), 216.

Voigt, C. (2009). *Sustainable development as a principle of international law: Resolving conflicts between climate measures and WTO law*. Martinus Nijhoff Publishers.

Weiss, E. B. (2019a). *Establishing norms in a Kaleidoscopic world—General course on public international law* (Vol. 396).

Weiss, E. B. (2019b). *General course on public international law* (Vol. 369).

WHO Framework Convention on Tobacco Control. (2017). *Guidelines for implementation of Article 6* (No. FCTC/16.7). Retrieved February 2, 2025, from https://fctc.who.int/resources/publications/m/item/price-and-tax-measures-to-reduce-the-demand-for-tobacco

Wolfrum, R. (2019). *Solidarity and community interests: Driving forces for the interpretation and development of international law* (Vol. 416). Brill Nijhoff.

Chapter 8
Can the Framework Tax Convention Reshape the Global Tax System? Challenges and Opportunities Going Forward

Abstract Exploring the prospects for the FTC's transformative potential, this chapter addresses North-South divides, consensus on cooperation needs, protocol challenges and opportunities, and integration of principles like equity into DTAs. It highlights challenges like complementarity with OECD work and the aspirational nature of principles, urging tangible outcomes beyond rhetoric.

8.1 North Versus South

The development of the FTC has consistently highlighted tensions between HICs and LMICs. The impetus for the FTC stems from the perception among LMICs that the OECD's de facto leadership of the international tax system inadequately addresses their needs. In his opening remarks, the Chair of the Ad Hoc Committee (Egypt), tasked with drafting the TOR, emphasised that international tax issues should be addressed 'in a manner that benefits all, with contributions from all nations, rather than permitting a few states or regional organisations to impose their rules'.[1] Similarly, The Bahamas remarked at the Ad Hoc Committee: 'For over six decades, international tax practices shaped and dictated by the OECD have failed to address the inherent challenges faced by the Global South'.[2]

During the TOR negotiations, OECD members sought to moderate the FTC's objectives, scope, and binding nature by advocating for decision-making by

[1] Opening remarks by Mr Ramy M Youssef to the First Session (26 April 2024) (n 44 in Chap. 2).

[2] UNGA Meetings Coverage (n 41 in Chap. 2) The Bahamas.

E. Vanderbruggen, *Reconstructing Global Tax Governance*, SpringerBriefs in Law, https://doi.org/10.1007/978-981-95-5617-5_8

consensus rather than majority,[3] emphasising complementarity[4] with existing frameworks, and prioritising DRM.[5] These members also expressed concerns that developing binding protocols at an early stage, without prior comprehensive technical analyses, would be premature.[6]

Predictably, LMICs would not entertain the OECD members' pushback on most of these issues. As was discussed above, one of the main triggers for the FTC is LMICs' discontent with the OECD leadership, process and outcomes. It is an attempted hostile takeover of the international tax rule-making system. In this type of undertaking, consent of existing stakeholders is unlikely to be sought, nor extended. Likewise, as another main driver is the longstanding dissatisfaction with the international taxing right distribution put in place at the insistence of the HICs, LMICs will not agree to shift the focus from their problems to their own flaws in running domestic tax systems.

The voting patterns for resolutions pertaining to the FTC reveal a marked international divergence of views. The FTC originated from resolutions that exposed a significant North-South divide, with evolving voting patterns highlighting contrasting priorities. Resolution 78/230,[7] adopted by the UN General Assembly's Second Committee on 22 December 2023, was a critical milestone, establishing the decision to create the FTC and launching the intergovernmental process to draft its TOR. The resolution garnered support from 125 Members, predominantly from the Global South, with the African Group at the forefront, advocating for a majority voting system to accelerate decision-making. In contrast, 48 states, primarily from the Global North—including the United States, United Kingdom, and other OECD members—opposed the resolution, expressing concerns over potential duplication

[3] European Union, 1st Meeting of the First Session (26 April 2024) (n 44 in Chap. 2); Hungary on behalf of the European Union, 1st Meeting of the Second Session (29 July 2024) (n 44 in Chap. 2); Canada on behalf of Canada, Australia and New Zealand, 1st Meeting of the Second Session (29 July 2024) (n 44 in Chap. 2); Canada, 4th Meeting of the First Session (29 April 2024) (n 44 in Chap. 2); The Netherlands, 1st Meeting of the Second Session (n 44 in Chap. 2).

[4] Republic of Korea, 2nd and 7th Meeting of the First Session (n 44 in Chap. 2); Czech Republic, 7th Meeting of the First Session (1 May 2024) (n 44 in Chap. 2); United States, 1st Meeting of the Second Session (29 July 2024) (n 44 in Chap. 2); Republic of Korea, 1st Meeting of the Second Session (29 July 2024) (n 44 in Chap. 2); Hungary on behalf of the European Union, 1st Meeting of the Second Session (29 July 2024) (n 44 in Chap. 2).

[5] Norway, 1st Meeting of the Second Session (29 July 2024) (n 44 in Chap. 2); Canada, 3rd Meeting of the Second Session (30 July 2024) (n 44 in Chap. 2); Japan, 3rd Meeting of the Second Session (30 July 2024) (n 44 in Chap. 2); Poland, 2nd Meeting of the First Session (26 April 2024) (n 44 in Chap. 2); Italy, 2nd Meeting of the First Session (26 April 2024) (n 44 in Chap. 2). In a way, HICs mean hereby that developing countries should not only look at taxing Multinational Enterprises (MNEs) but also broaden their national tax base, improve tax transparency and get better at taxing the wealthy in their countries (more on this later).

[6] Hungary on behalf of the EU, Inputs to the Second Session (n 44 in Chap. 2); Japan, Inputs to the First Session (n 44 in Chap. 2).

[7] United Nations General Assembly (UNGA) (2023).

of existing frameworks, such as the OECD's IF. Nine states, including Türkiye, abstained, reflecting more nuanced positions.[8]

Subsequent negotiations in 2024 culminated in the adoption of the TOR for the FTC on 16 August 2024,[9] with 110 states voting in favour, 44 abstaining, and eight—Australia, Canada, Israel, Japan, New Zealand, Republic of Korea, United Kingdom, and United States—opposing.[10] This voting pattern reflects a reduction in outright opposition compared to prior resolutions, though the increase in abstentions suggests persistent reservations among some HICs.

The voting patterns underscore a pronounced North-South divide, with the Global South advocating for inclusive and binding reforms to tackle tax evasion and challenges posed by the digital economy, while the Global North prioritises the preservation of existing frameworks, such as the OECD's IF. The progression from 2023 to 2024 indicates incremental steps towards consensus; however, significant tensions remain, as evidenced by the United States' announcement of its withdrawal from the discussions.

The organisational session of the INC for the FTC, convened from 3–6 February 2025 at UN Headquarters in New York, addressed pivotal procedural matters, reflecting the enduring divide between the Global North and Global South. As mandated by UN General Assembly Resolution 79/235, the session aimed to establish the INC's work programme and finalise operational frameworks for negotiations spanning 2025–2027. A central point of contention was the decision-making threshold. The African Group, alongside other Global South states, advocated for majority voting to prevent minority vetoes, emphasising the need for inclusive and equitable global tax governance. In contrast, most HICs supported consensus-based decision-making to ensure broad acceptance and effective implementation, citing risks of fragmenting existing international tax frameworks.

The outcome is a hybrid decision-making model: a two-thirds majority for substantive issues and a simple majority for procedural matters in the absence of consensus, as delineated in the INC's organisational decisions. This compromise facilitates progress in negotiations but underscores persistent tensions, exemplified by the United States' withdrawal from the session, which signals distrust in the process or perhaps more a reluctance in general to participate in international approaches to regulating taxation. The African Group's leadership stressed the necessity of inclusive procedures to address challenges faced by LMICs, such as tax base erosion, while HICs underscored the importance of national sovereignty and alignment with established OECD frameworks. These discussions highlight the evolving North-South divide, with incremental advancements in procedural clarity but ongoing challenges in achieving substantive consensus.

One of the issues where the North-South divide is most felt is the problem of the complementarity of the FTC with the OECD work in the international tax space.

---

[8] United Nations (2023).

[9] United Nations General Assembly (UNGA) (2024).

[10] UNGA A/79/333 (n 2 in Chap. 1).

HICs repeatedly pushed for some kind of recognition that the FTC would not venture into areas already subject of international cooperation led by the G20 and OECD's IF. However, the Ad Hoc Committee would not adopt a rule that would put its work in a permanent subsidiary role to the OECD. Nevertheless, a sufficient legal basis remains for the FTC to build in working with or deferring to OECD outcomes.[11]

The FTC's proposed framework may complement OECD accomplishments in practice, despite ongoing UN negotiations. The OECD's extensive work in international taxation remains significant, and duplicating it offers little value unless justified by gaps in universally accepted solutions. The FTC's initial protocols, particularly on source taxation of services and digital income, and resolution of tax disputes, are target areas where the OECD, Inclusive Framework, or Global Forum has not yet achieved broad consensus, particularly among LMICs. The 2025 prioritization of a protocol on cross-border services highlights the OECD's challenges in securing universal support on its Pillar One solution. However, the FTC's success in addressing these issues remains uncertain, given similar consensus challenges.

With these caveats, it seems that the practical effects of the OECD's work on FTC outcomes will remain the reality for many years. In a way, it is possible that international tax cooperation will be more prominently 'co-chaired' than has been the case to date, at least for some time.

8.2 Areas of Substantial Consensus

Certain issues in the FTC's proposed framework reflect broad state agreement, despite ongoing negotiations. For example, it seems generally accepted, even at the Ad Hoc Committee, that international cooperation on a wide range of tax matters is indeed necessary. Even well before the process towards the FTC was undertaken, HICs and LMICs alike do not contest the fact that the world increasingly faces tax problems that can only or most effectively be addressed through international cooperation. Issues such as tax evasion and information exchange, the need to evolve rules on taxing rights to keep up with technological developments, taxation of multinational enterprises, BEPS and harmful tax practices are intrinsically difficult to tackle via unilateral or bilateral approaches, even with fewer political obstacles.[12] The OECD-led projects and the wide membership of the IF in the LMICs underscore this. The forces of globalization and technology have created a world where international tax cooperation is necessary, not optional. The work by the OECD and the IF underscores that technology, multinational enterprises and high-net worth individuals, financial secrecy havens, BEPS and harmful tax practices are intrinsically difficult or impossible to tackle via unilateral or bilateral approaches, even

[11] United Nations General Assembly (UNGA) (2024), para 6 states that the FTC should reflect Resolutions 78/230 and 77/244, which both address the issue of complementarity. Also, para 22 refers explicitly to possible complementarities.

[12] Cui (2020), p. 260; Picciotto (2017), pp. 5–22; Avi-Yonah and Mazzoni (2018), p. 885.

among the more likeminded,[13] and for some of these challenges, even within the EU.[14] Despite the occasional political rhetoric to the contrary, it seems the awareness has taken hold that it is not effective or even possible to orderly manage the worlds' tax affairs only with unilateralist and bilateralist approaches.

Thus, the question is not whether international cooperation is needed, but whether it should be multilateral and OECD-led or international and UN-grounded. Multilateral initiatives have been successful in fostering cooperation on global economic issues, but the multipolar international context is challenging. Perhaps the WTO is the best illustration of this change. Compared to a few decades ago, the WTO presently faces difficult questions related to efficacy.[15] At the present time, bilateral, regional and plurilateral efforts, illustrated by digital FTAs, mega-regionals like the Comprehensive and Progressive Agreement for Trans-Pacific Partnership (CPTPP) and the Regional Comprehensive Economic Partnership (RCEP), and special cooperation such as the Multi-Party Interim Appeal Arbitration Arrangement (MPIA) and the Agreement on Climate Change, Trade and Sustainability (ACCTS), step in at the legislative, regulatory and judicial levels of international relations where progress at a WTO level seems elusive.

Furthermore, at the Ad Hoc Committee, it seems no state was opposed to the UN as an appropriate forum to play a key role in international tax cooperation. Even OECD members were not opposed, provided it would be complementary to the OECD's existing work. Most States furthermore agreed that on certain issues, the UN is in a unique institutional position to make progress, for example in relation to international transportation with both the IMO and the ICAO within its orbit.[16]

While there is some consensus that the UN is an appropriate forum for international tax cooperation and may assume an enhanced role, different views remain on whether there should be ipso facto complementarity regarding all OECD outcomes. However, as was mentioned above, this does not exclude complementarity in actual practice. Furthermore, the negotiations at the Ad Hoc Committee indicate that several of the objectives, principles and commitments of the TOR are as a matter of principle not controversial between HICs and LMICs. There is agreement in broad strokes that the international tax system needs to be responsive to the fundamental goals of the international community such as international equity and the financing of sustainable development. There is also agreement that all states should be able to fully participate in rulemaking, that international tax cooperation should be aligned with human rights obligations and that DRM be a key objective of international tax cooperation. Furthermore, there is consensus that there should be international

[13] Ibid.

[14] See for example the EU state aid dispute between the Commission and Ireland in connection with the tax treatment of Apple: Case C-465/20 P *Commission v Ireland and Others* EU:C:2024:724.

[15] In 1947, there were many connections and relationships between the UN and founding of the GATT (n 5 in Chap. 5), but as Neumann finds, the commencement of the Cold War played a major role in the General Agreement becoming an international organization in its own right and not a specialized agency of the UN: Neumann (1970), pp. 63, 78.

[16] France, Inputs to the First Session (n 44 in Chap. 2).

cooperation, including high-level and specific commitments, to curb international tax evasion and aggressive avoidance, improve transparency and address IFF. Finally, it seems uncontroversial for the FTC to provide (mostly non-binding) international means to settle tax disputes in connection with the convention.

These are significant departures from the unilateralism and bilateralism that have characterized international taxation for most of its history. Codifying the above in a binding framework convention, even as principles and high-level commitments, with binding protocols likely to be acceptable on a plurilateral basis, even lacking universality, would constitute a significant progression of the global tax system.

Although they may look for different applications and outcomes (at times even of the same principle), the OECD, the UN and virtually all the states represented at the Ad Hoc Committee do share the view that international tax cooperation must reflect certain values that are fundamental to the community. Indeed, principles of fairness or equity also, to some extent, underpin the BEPS Project, the Global Forum and the MLC on Mutual Administrative Assistance in Tax Matters, but with outcomes perhaps less oriented towards the balance of taxing rights between source and residence.[17] Thus, it does not seem to be controversial that international cooperation is needed, nor is it an open question whether certain values should be a part of the reconsideration of the existing system, which puts into perspective the 'every man for himself' approach to global tax affairs. From the discussions at the Ad Hoc Committee there is some agreement -even with many OECD members- that tax cooperation should perhaps not exclusively be multilateral and OECD-led in nature, but can also be international and UN-grounded.[18]

8.3 Thoughts on the Protocols

Some Framework conventions have a strong track record for fostering international consensus through protocols with binding obligations.[19] It is noteworthy that the subjects for the protocols have deliberately been left to be defined in detail by the

---

[17] Multilateral Convention on Mutual Administrative Assistance in Tax Matters amended by the 2010 Protocol (signed 27 May 2010, entered into force 1 June 2011).

[18] See for example the Written Inputs to the First Session (United Nations 2024a) of the OECD members the UK, Denmark, Estonia, France, Germany, Finland, and Italy, referring to the UN's broad membership, strengths or legitimacy.

[19] UNFCCC (n 39 in Chap. 2) (198 member states); FCTC (n 1 in Chap. 4) (183 parties); Convention on Prohibitions or Restrictions on the Use of Certain Conventional Weapons which may be deemed to be Excessively Injurious or to have Indiscriminate Effects (signed 10 April 1981, entered into force 2 December 1983) 1342 UNTS 137 (128 parties); CBD (n 4 in Chap. 6) (196 parties); CLRTAP (n 3 in Chap. 4) (51 parties—note that this convention focuses on the European continent); Convention for the Protection of the Mediterranean Sea against Pollution (opened for signature 16 February 1976, entered into force 16 February 1976) 1102 UNTS 27 (22 states around the Mediterranean sea).

FTC drafters, resulting in freedom for the states to find room for specific measures that fit under the flag of that subject matter.

For example, from the negotiations at the Ad Hoc Committee, binding obligations under one or more protocols on tax evasion, IFF, mutual assistance and the exchange of information are not controversial, because many states consider addressing these issues a priority. The options to advance binding obligations on these issues are vast, and perhaps a primary issue is that the complementarity with the Global Forum and Multilateral Convention on Mutual Administrative Assistance in Tax Matters will have to be worked out. However, enhancing the effectiveness of these already successful initiatives can be fertile ground for a protocol. For instance, this can be achieved by establishing obligations to mitigate reciprocity or by providing international assistance with data safeguards and resource constraints. More self-contained examples would be public CbC reporting,[20] disclosure of the beneficial owners of special purpose vehicles or a 'global high value asset registry'.[21]

A second example is in the cooperation to tax ultra-high-net-worth individuals, which was generally supported by the Ad Hoc Committee. Again, numerous possible measures may be considered in this regard, including the noteworthy exploration by Brazil as part of its G20 Presidency of a 2% annual baseline tax for billionaires.[22]

Another example, namely the planned protocol for the settlement of tax disputes, might find support if it provides non-binding means for all states (as does the UNFCCC) and binding arbitration in relation to taxpayers only for those states that already accept arbitration on double taxation[23] or for tax-related investment claims.

The FTC may include a provision on the settlement of disputes like other framework conventions, probably using non-binding methods. A combination of consultations and (sometimes compulsory) conciliation with a body of experts or a commission composed of equal numbers of members from each party and the power to make 'advisory' awards may be acceptable to many states.[24] A more ambitious target would be creating new commitments with respect to tax-related investment disputes, as per the observation in Resolution 78/230, for example, by organizing financial assistance and capacity. By now, a long list of investment claims has been decided, of which the domestic tax treatment of a foreign investor was the basis.[25] Possibly, although unlikely, the FTC would address this issue, if only to secure funding and capacity building.

---

[20] In a manner similar to the Council Directive (EU) 2021/2101 of 24 November 2021 amending Directive 2013/34/EU of the European Parliament and of the Council as regards disclosure of income tax information by certain undertakings and branches; IBFD inputs (n 44 in Chap. 2).

[21] Pakistan, Columbia and Senegal, Second Session, 4th Meeting of the Second Session (30 July 2024) (n 44 in Chap. 2); Columbia, 6th Meeting of the Second Session (31 July 2024) (n 44 in Chap. 2).

[22] Zucman (2024).

[23] As was illustrated in the responses to the OECD (2017), art 19.

[24] UNFCCC (n 39 in Chap. 2) art 14. See also, Bodansky (1999), p. 27.

[25] UNCTAD (n 59 in Chap. 6) 5; Peters (1995), pp. 45, 52.

It would be challenging—but not impossible—for the FTC to have a game-changing impact on international tax disputes. The prevention and resolution of tax disputes having been chosen as the second early protocol[26] illustrates that several states find binding measures on dispute settlement logical and important. The OECD MLI attempted to introduce mandatory binding arbitration.[27] However, few LMICs have accepted binding arbitration in bilateral DTAs, though some may reconsider their stance within the FTC's proposed multilateral framework, where benefits like capacity building, exchange of information, enhanced taxing rights, and source taxation on services could foster broader agreement. While binding arbitration in bilateral DTAs offers advantages for LMICs, it requires mutual acceptance by both states. In contrast, an FTC protocol's multilateral cross-benefits may more effectively encourage state participation. For Korea, 'in the case of Korea, we are not supportive of mandatory mediation or arbitration. However, in terms of enhancing tax certainty, we are open to discussing these issues'.[28]

Cross-border services, the subject of the first early protocol, are controversial among HICs and LMICs.[29] Again, the Ad Hoc Committee intentionally steered away from defining the subject[30] and from clarifying the potential overlap with 'taxation of the digitalized economy'. Numerous approaches are therefore possible. A possibility is a protocol establishing source taxation on all cross-border services, which may be acceptable to a significant and growing number of states.[31] The protocol might then serve as a vehicle to facilitate the swift amendment of DTAs for agreeable states and to keep up with the next wave of technological developments.[32] However, the controversial nature of cross-border services makes universal consensus unlikely.

A final example, international cooperation on environmental taxes, was regularly mentioned during the Ad Hoc Committee by both HICs and LMICs.[33] It is likely that among the wide spectrum of potential measures, some would be agreeable to numerous states.

---

[26] International Institute for Sustainable Development (IISD) (n.d.).

[27] OECD (2017), art 19; Noonan and Plekhanova (2023).

[28] Korea, 6th Meeting of the First Session (30 April 2024) (n 44 in Chap. 2).

[29] United Nations General Assembly (UNGA) (2024), para 15: 'taxation of income derived from the provision of cross-border services in an increasingly digitalized and globalized economy'.

[30] South Africa, 12th Meeting of the First Session (3 May 2024) (n 44 in Chap. 2).

[31] According to the International Bureau of Fiscal Documentation, a significant number of DTAs contains source taxation on fees for technical services, notably 40% of non-OECD/non-OECD DTAs, 22% of non-OECD/OECD DTAs and 8% of OECD/OECD DTAs. This data was based on the period between 2010 and 2023: IBFD Inputs (n 44 in Chap. 2).

[32] The UN Committee of Experts in International Tax, prepared in 2023, a 'Fast Track Instrument' aimed at amending existing tax treaties to help implement UN Model DTA provisions with more room for taxation at source: Co-Coordinators' Report (n 16 in Chap. 3).

[33] For example, France indicated that this may be a fruitful avenue to focus on: France, Inputs to the First Session (n 44 in Chap. 2).

8.4 Transcending the Silo of International Tax Law

While the existing international tax system to some extent reflects certain community interests and principles like fairness and cooperation, the FTC's explicit adoption of inclusivity, equity, sustainable development, and human rights as foundational principles marks a novel advance in international tax law. This development aligns with the emerging recognition of climate and human rights imperatives and their implications for the rights and obligations of States under international law in matters of taxation. As was argued above, the advisory opinion of the ICJ on climate change, alongside the pronouncements of other international courts underscore that States are obligated under conventional and customary international law, with a margin of appreciation or discretion, to ensure the fiscal adequacy of their domestic climate or human rights measures, including, within their national circumstances, to undertake tax reforms and target potential tax resources when necessary.[34] The FTC seeks to bridge the disconnect between climate, human rights, and development objectives and the fiscal means to achieve them, by embedding principles like sustainable development, equity, and human rights into international tax governance. A key question is the potential significance of this development to the international law of taxation.

Given the prominent position of DTAs in the present network of international tax rules, and the criticism associated with the balance of taxing power established by DTAs, it is appropriate to examine whether the proposed core principles of the FTC will reverberate throughout the international tax system through the interpretation of not only the FTC and its protocols but also independent tax- and tax-related treaties, particularly DTAs. The firmly established principle of systematic integration reflected in art. 31 (3) (c) VCLT requires the interpreter of a treaty to take into account 'any relevant rules of international law applicable in the relations between the parties' which are external to the treaty itself.[35] Consequently, 'applicability' and 'relevance' are crucial threshold requirements before an extraneous rule of law can be considered for determining the meaning of a treaty term.

Applicability in the sense of Art. 31 (3) (c) VCLT, requires that the principles set out in the FTC are legally binding on all the parties to a treaty, in this case for example a DTA.[36] To have such effect, it is crucial that several of the objectives and principles that are adopted by Resolution 79/235 constitute or overlap with one or more legal norms found in treaties or in general international law. The applicability of certain human rights obligations under general international law is well

[34] See several sections

[35] *Oil Platforms case (Iran v USA)* (Merits) [2003] ICJ Rep 161 (*Oil Platforms*), para 41; *Right of Passage over Indian Territory (Portugal v India)* (Merits) [1957] ICJ Rep 125, 142; *Georges Pinson (France) v United Mexican States* (Decision of 19 October 1928) [1928] UNRIAA 327, 422; ITLOS *Climate Change Advisory Opinion* (n 34 in Chap. 7), paras 128–137; McLachlan (2024); McLachlan (2005), pp. 279, 293; International Law Commission (ILC) (2006c), p. 413.

[36] Villiger (2009), p. 433, para 25.

established. It is not in doubt that several human rights protections found in the Universal Declaration and the Covenants[37] are binding on and a concern to the international community (*erga omnes*).[38] Furthermore, while the legal status (or applicability) of sustainable development *per se* has been debated or intentionally unaddressed by scholars,[39] from the analysis above it seems clear there has been a progressive development towards enhanced normativity, culminating in the 2025 ICJ AO including sustainable development as a legal principle encompassed in the applicable law concerning climate change.[40] Finally, as was examined above, the legal principle of equity has been invoked in several decisions of the ICJ.[41] However, as the ICJ confirmed explicitly in its advisory opinion on climate change, one can rely on equity as a guiding principle *infra legem*, not *contra legem*.[42]

With respect to the question of relevance, tax may be directly relevant to SDGs,[43] impacting them positively or negatively, as is the case with tax subsidies or carbon tax pricing of fossil fuels,[44] the role of tax in tobacco control,[45] or discriminatory taxes on women.[46] However, it is fair to say that to the participants of the international tax system, for the most part tax officials, taxpayers (and their advisors) and municipal tax courts, the core principles proposed by the FTC seem distanced from daily operation of DTAs, constituting the bulk of the international rules. While considerations of fairness or equity underpin certain broader multilateral initiatives meant to address specific problems such as transfer pricing, transparency and BEPS, and these are even (sometimes) acknowledged as such, they have not usually been credited with much or any normative content for the application of international tax rules.[47] Much of the understandable precaution in connecting "vague" principles such as sustainable development or fairness or equity to the rather mechanical and transactional universe of DTAs relate to relevance.

Another way of approaching relevance is through *lex specialis derogat lex generalis*. Does a DTA comprise obligations which are *lex specialis* to obligations

[37] ICCPR (n 11 in Chap. 7); ICESCR (n 11 in Chap. 7).

[38] Preamble of the UDHR (n 12 in Chap. 7); see also *Reservations on Genocide* (n 12 in Chap. 7); *Convention on Genocide* (n 12 in Chap. 7); *Barcelona Traction, Light and Power Company, Limited (Belgium v Spain)* [1970] (Merits) ICJ Rep 3, para 33.

[39] As noted by Beyerlin (2013), p. 15 (this entry was last updated in October 2013).

[40] International Court of Justice (ICJ) (2025), para 147.

[41] See above Sect. 7.3.

[42] International Court of Justice (ICJ) (2025), paras 152–154.

[43] UNGA Res 70/1 (n 25 in Chap. 1).

[44] Kyoto Protocol (n 16 in Chap. 7) art 2(1)(v).

[45] FCTC (n 1 in Chap. 4) art 6(2).

[46] See for example the comments by the Committee created under the CEDAW (n 164 in Chap. 7): CEDAW (2016), paras 40–43; CEDAW (2018), paras 10, 15, 16.

[47] OECD (2013), pp. 8, 15 (referring to fairness in international taxation); OECD TPG (n 71 in Chap. 6), para 4.27 (referring to fairness in imposing penalties). One finds significantly more references in materials that are not meant to have legal effects on tax imposition rules, such as in OECD (2024).

stemming from human rights, sustainable development or the duty of cooperation? That is conceivable, perhaps, but on a norm-by-norm basis and not as a general carve-out for every and any subject matter that is covered by the DTA. For example, one could argue that Art. 24 OECD Model DTA provides in a very special and limited form of anti-discrimination, notably applicable only to a less favorable income tax treatment by a State of nationals of the other State that are in the same circumstance in terms of their tax residence. This may indeed constitute *lex specialis* for that particular kind of discrimination. Art. 24 would not be able to displace for example the National Treatment provision of investment agreements, featuring the duty not to discriminate foreign nationals more in general.[48] Even in the case of *lex specialis*, the external norm does not expire. As was made clear in *Military and Paramilitary Activities*, the extraneous norm remains valid and applicable, may influence the interpretation and may even come to the forefront as a gap filler.[49] Rules from different areas of law can nevertheless be relevant as the ICJ confirmed in *Oil Platforms,* where the Court relied on art. 31 (3) (c) VCLT to take into account the general international law on the use of force to help define a commercial and economic treaty.[50] What matters is that the rule concerns the subject-matter of the treaty term at issue.[51] Therefore, even though sustainable development or fairness or equity have a broad nature, it can nevertheless be "relevant" in the sense of art. 31 (3) (c) VCLT. This was confirmed in *Mutual Assistance in Criminal Matters*,[52] where the ICJ considered fundamental rules on "equality" and "cooperation" in a 1977 treaty which are obviously 'formulated in a broad and general manner, having an aspirational character' had to be taken into account to interpret relevant to a 1986 treaty on cooperation in criminal matters.[53]

However, applicability and relevance alone do not guarantee a different outcome pursuant to contextual interpretation. Art. 31 (3) (c) VCLT mandates the interpreter to take applicable relevant rules into account, together with the context, but it does not prioritize those extraneous rules over, for instance, the ordinary meaning of treaty provisions. Tax rules, particularly the substantive tax provisions in DTAs, are most often characterized by their utilitarian nature. The participants of the international tax system apply these rules on a daily basis and a high degree of certainty and predictability is thus a basic requirement. The substantive provisions of DTAs typically provide in rather mechanical, closed-textured and straightforward distributive clauses assigning taxing authority to one or the other state, and in an obligation to provide a credit. DTA clauses are by no means always self-explanatory, but

[48] The common carve-out for certain tax measures from National Treatment reflects *lex specialis*.

[49] *Military and Paramilitary Activities in and against Nicaragua (Nicaragua v US)* [1986] (Merits) ICJ Rep 14, para 179.

[50] *Oil Platforms* (n 35 in this chapter), para 41. See also *Oil Platforms* (n 35 in this chapter) Separate Opinion of Judge Higgins, para 46.

[51] See also the statements by Tunkin and Waldock (1964), p. 310; Ago (1970), pp. 177, 192–193.

[52] *Certain Questions of Mutual Assistance in Criminal Matters (Djibouti v France)* (Merits) [2008] ICJ Rep 177 (*Mutual Assistance*), para 112.

[53] Ibid, para 113.

keeping in mind the pronouncements of the ICJ in its AO on Climate Change, legal principles such as equity and sustainable development are meant to guide rather than displace other norms, in this case the normativity of the DTAs' distributive clauses.[54] In addition, it should be noted that DTAs lack some of the textual basis found in more open-textured treaties such as trade agreements and investment agreements to incorporate environmental or human rights concerns. Indeed, several agreements refer explicitly in their preamble or body to environmental concerns and legitimate (public) policy objectives, for example in connection to a 'right to regulate' or general exceptions.[55] Such references are only very rarely found in DTAs, if at all.

Equity and sustainable development, while constituting legal principles, do not offer the degree of detailed normativity that can alter existing tax rules. Indeed, while sustainable development and fairness or equity is enshrined in numerous treaties[56] and invoked in cases before international courts and tribunals in certain circumstances,[57] their application in the context of establishing an international tax system—beyond rhetoric—remains undeveloped. As the ICJ AO confirms, the legal principle of equity employed by the FTC does not function as a displacement of treaty norms but 'to derive an equitable solution as appropriate from the applicable law'.[58] Similarly, sustainable development informs the interpretation of treaties and identification of customary norms, rather than constituting an independent legal obligation.[59] The mere assertion of these principles within the FTC is, in itself,

---

[54] International Court of Justice (ICJ) (2025), paras 147 and 153.

[55] For example, GATT (n 5 in Chap. 5) art XX; Free Trade Agreement between Canada and the Republic of Korea (signed 22 September 2014, entered into force 1 January 2015) art 17.2; Advanced Framework Agreement between the European Union and the Republic of Chile (signed 13 December 2023) (EU-Chile AFA) art 18.3; Investment Protection Agreement between the European Union and its Member States, of the one part, and Singapore, of the other part (signed 15 October 2018) (EU—Singapore IPA) art 2.2.1; Investment Protection Agreement between the European Union and its Member States, of the one part, and Viet Nam, of the other part (signed 30 June 2019) (EU—Viet Nam IPA) art 2.2.1; Comprehensive Economic and Trade Agreement between Canada, of the one part, and the European Union and its Member States, of the other part (signed 30 October 2016, entered into force 21 September 2017) (CETA) arts 8.9.1, 15.14; TCA (n 45 in Chap. 7) art 123(1)(2); similarly, Comprehensive and Progressive Agreement for Trans-Pacific Partnership (signed 8 March 2018, entered into force 30 December 2018) (CPTPP) Chapters 25, 29 (footnote 5); USMCA (n 53 in Chap. 7) preamble; Regional Comprehensive Economic Partnership (signed 15 November 2020, entered into force 1 January 2022) (RCEP) art 17.12 (footnote 5).

[56] As referred in the climate treaties: UNFCCC (n 39 in Chap. 2) art 3(4); Kyoto Protocol (n 16 in Chap. 7) art 2(1); Paris Agreement (n 10 in Chap. 5) art 2(1), rather than as a 'concept' in *Gabčíkovo-Nagymaros* (n 19 in Chap. 4), para 140; Brundtland (1987) 43; United Nations (1992); UNGA Res 60/1 (n 46 in Chap. 7), para 48; United Nations General Assembly (UNGA) (2024), para 9(d); UNGA Res 70/1 (n 25 in Chap. 1).

[57] See *North Sea Continental Shelf* (n 93 in Chap. 7), para 85; *Continental Shelf* (n 105 in Chap. 7), para 71; *Loan Agreement* (n 105 in Chap. 7), para 69.

[58] International Court of Justice (ICJ) (2025), para 153.

[59] International Court of Justice (ICJ) (2025), para 147.

insufficient to effectuate changes to treaty norms governing taxation. Whereas the connection between taxation and human rights is widely recognized, even if one accepts that states are under legal obligation to ensure the adequacy of their national tax system to finance human rights, which arguably can be deduced from the recent pronouncements of international courts, this has yet to be explicitly confirmed and consequently, the deference for the state in making fiscal policy renders it challenging to evaluate whether states have violated such obligation.

With or without explicit reference in the preamble or text, it seems that the core principles of the FTC have only a limited space to in and of themselves displace the frequently mechanical substantive content of DTAs (tax) treaties. Even with art. 31 (3) (c) VCLT, an external rule of international law cannot make a DTA say what it does not say. Extraneous rules or legal principles (and objectives) are unlikely to push aside unambiguous and conclusive treaty rules.[60] A DTA provision providing in a maximum percentage for a withholding tax, or a lack of taxing rights on airline or shipping profits, or capital gains, leaves little room for contextual interpretation. Certainly, the application of various DTA rules may be uncertain and disputed between the taxpayers and tax authorities, for example in connection with the definition of a permanent establishment, the identification of a beneficial owner, an arm's length prices or profit, or whether an income is connected to a permanent establishment. But it does not seem that such technical and utilitarian tax questions would benefit much from an infusion of extraneous meaning. It is relevant that many of the relevant DTAs' legal concepts have been defined for decades by conventional and soft norms applicable or familiar to the State parties to DTAs. Even a rule of general international law can be derogated from by parties to a tax-related treaty provided it does not constitute *jus cogens.*[61] The prospects for invoking external rules to DTAs is likely less limited where treaty rules are silent or use terms that are meant to be infused with exogenous meaning.[62]

The invocation of sustainable development, equity and human rights by the FTC stands in contrast to the predominantly voluntarist and bilateralist nature of the 1920s compromise and its legacy, governed mainly by DTAs and certain OECD-led multilateral departures. In an era of international law where community interests and human-centric approaches are clearly on the rise[63] it seems improbable that it is possible let alone legitimate to continue to carve-out taxation from this development.

[60] WTO, *EC Measures Concerning Meat and Meat Products (Hormones) – Complaint by the United States – Report of the Panel* (18 August 1997) WT/DS26/R/USA, paras 8.157–8.158; WTO, *EC Measures Concerning Meat and Meat Products (Hormones) – Complaint by Canada – Report of the Panel* (18 August 1997) WT/DS48/R/CAN, paras 8.160–8.161; *Vattenfall AB and others v Federal Republic of Germany,* ICSID Case No ARB/12/12, Decision on the Achmea Issue (31 August 2018), paras 154, 205; similarly, *Eskosol SpA in liquidazione v Italian Republic,* ICSID Case No ARB/15/50, Decision on Termination Request and Intra-EU Objection (7 May 2019), para 126; *RENERGY Sàrl v Kingdom of Spain,* ICSID Case No ARB/14/18, Award (6 May 2022), para 370; Handl (1995), p. 35; Hill (2023), p. 244.

[61] VCLT (n 1 in Chap. 4) arts 53 and 64.

[62] Wolfrum (2019), p. 126.

[63] Simma (1994), p. 234.

The alternative post-sovereigntist conceptualization of the international law of taxation, reflected in the FTC, is still fuzzy. It is reasonable to approach it with caution. As the rationale for the FTC acknowledges, a new international tax system aimed at sustainable development and based on fairness or equity will require more than just the systemically integrated interpretation of the rules we already have, for which the utilitarian, closed-textured substantive rules of DTAs seem to leave little room. But even in the present tentative state of an international tax system beyond voluntarism, the forces of globalization, the humanization of international law and the operationalization of universal values render it unlikely that one can continue to artificially isolate taxation. Even at this stage it seems taxation is too pervasive in the international system to persist legally detached and self-contained, "La Belle Au Bois Dormant",[64] in splendid isolation from these fundamental shifts that are changing international law. The international legal system is a system,[65] and the participants' rights and obligations in tax matters should not and are not quarantined from the rest of it.

8.5 From Abstract Principles to Tangible Outcomes

It is worth noting that the FTC represents a departure from the FCCC, arguably the most prominent framework convention to date in its approach to attaching equitable principles to the subject matter of a framework convention.[66] From the outset, the FCCC's INC clearly embraced the principle of differentiation, grounded in fairness.[67] This principle drew partial inspiration from GA Resolution 45/212, adopted without a vote, which declared in its preamble that HICs, as the primary polluters, bear the main responsibility for combating pollution.[68] It was generally accepted that pollution resulted from industrialization, making it equitable to hold highly industrialized states to greater accountability. Consequently, in the case of the FCCC there was an agreement between parties on sustainable development and fairness as foundational principles, and these were reflected in the treaty. In contrast, the FTC does the reverse. As universal consensus on some of the key questions affecting the international tax system remains elusive, the FTC is reflecting these principles in the treaty in the hope it may encourage agreement.[69]

As was pointed out in the analysis above, taxation is connected to virtually everything as the most important financing tool for sustainable development,

[64] The classic tale of "Sleeping Beauty", attributed to Perrault and Grimm (n.d.).

[65] International Law Commission (ILC) (2006a); International Law Commission (ILC) (2006b), para 251.

[66] UNFCCC (n 39 in Chap. 2).

[67] Bodansky et al. (2017), p. 121; see also United Nations (1992), principle 7.

[68] United Nations General Assembly (UNGA) (1990), preamble recital 8.

[69] On the effects of principles see Dworkin (1977), p. 24.

climate action and human rights objectives. International cooperation on SDGs without international cooperation on taxation makes about as much sense as building a car without an engine.

A reconsideration of some of the premises of the international tax system, already foreshadowed by Klaus Vogel writing in the eighties,[70] may be overdue. As Vella concludes "much is wrong with the international business tax system. It is economically inefficient, susceptible to profit shifting, perceived by many to be unfair, difficult to comply with and administer, and incentive incompatible".[71] To which degree taxation, perhaps the last great bastion of sovereignty and voluntarism, will be reshaped by international norms reflecting community interests provokes the yet unresolved question of the fragmentation of international law and the global tax system. One vision for the international tax system is that bilateral transactional approaches to taxing rights are largely sufficient and that it does not need an influx of 'vague' principles that are according to the proponents of this approach are not relevant to tax imposition rules.

The opinions of international courts on climate change illustrate the emerging and progressively expanding constructive integration of international law into States' sovereign authority to design and administer national tax systems. The FTC aligns with this evolution, reinforcing the relevance of legal norms such as sustainable development, equity, and human rights within the international tax regime.

The most ambitious and commendable feature of the FTC also represents its principal limitation: applying the principles it proposes as the basis for a new international tax system is presently largely aspirational, lacking universal consensus and falling short of summoning the degree of normativity required to change existing tax rules. While the IACtHR underscored the potential for States to coordinate their national tax systems,[72] the FTCs approach to suggest alignment of international taxing rights with states' ability to finance human rights objectives, while a necessary and commendable first step, is insufficient.

The FTC must extend beyond merely affirming that the international tax system ought to align with principles such as sustainable development, fairness, and human rights, precisely because of the limited consensus on how to operationalize these principles into concrete outcomes. As The Netherlands put it: 'Member states have different opinions of what fair and equitable would be'.[73] The absence of a more detailed principled framework undermines its ambition to serve as a blueprint for equitable taxing rights. Despite concrete proposals for enhancing global justice in taxation,[74] there is a risk the FTC remains mired in abstract principles without practical progress. An area of relative clarity is the recognition that less-than-fully

[70] Vogel (1988).

[71] Vella (2025), p. 596 (at the time of writing this is an advance publication).

[72] IACtHR AO (n 161 in Chap. 7), para 263.

[73] Written inputs Second Session (n 44 in Chap. 2) Korea, The Netherlands, Portugal, Switzerland, US.

[74] Pogge and Mehtha (2016), p. 43.

inclusive participation in global tax rulemaking may be problematic, but even that should not exclude plurilateral advancement where universal consensus is tenuous. Without clearer guidance the FTC's objective of achieving a fair and equitable international tax system for sustainable development risks remaining elusive. Additional, targeted measures are essential to transition from abstract principles to tangible outcomes, particularly those that benefit individuals, as their interests are the primary focus of international measures aimed at advancing SDGs and human rights.[75]

In this regard, it may be more feasible to target novel taxable assets, those that may become available through innovative international instruments. For example, as the G20 recognized in 2024, taxing the migratory ultra-rich may be most efficient via international cooperation (such as common minimum standards and the coordination of exit taxes,).[76] Similarly, the taxation of fossil fuels used in international transportation is difficult to achieve with isolated domestic measures as vessels and aircraft can take on fuel in different countries.[77] These proposals and suggestions underscore that additional, targeted measures are essential to transition the FTC from abstract principles to tangible outcomes. However, addressing deficiencies in domestic tax systems remain the more critical mechanism, reflected in the objectives of the FTC through the concept of DRM.[78]

Case Law

Barcelona Traction, Light and Power Company, Limited (Belgium v Spain), ICJ Reports 3 (1970).

Certain Questions of Mutual Assistance in Criminal Matters (Djibouti v France), ICJ Reports 177 (2008).

Commission v Ireland and Others, Case No. C-465/20 P (Court of Justice of the European Union 2024).

EC Measures Concerning Meat and Meat Products (Hormones) – Complaint by Canada – Report of the Panel, No. WT/DS48/R/CAN (WTO August 18, 1997).

EC Measures Concerning Meat and Meat Products (Hormones) – Complaint by the United States – Report of the Panel, No. WT/DS26/R/USA (WTO).

Eskosol SpA in Liquidazione v Italian Republic, Case No. ARB/15/50 (ICSID May 7, 2019).

Georges Pinson (France) v United Mexican States, UNRIAA 327 (1928).

Military and Paramilitary Activities in and against Nicaragua (Nicaragua v US), ICJ Reports 14 (1986).

---

[75] Klabbers (2024), p. 312.

[76] Group of Twenty (G20) (2024), para 20; Zucman (2024), pp. 31–32.

[77] CE Delft (2022).

[78] United Nations General Assembly (UNGA) (2024), para 7(c); G20 Note (n 25 in Chap. 4).

Oil Platforms Case (Iran v USA), ICJ Reports 161 (2003).
RENERGY Sàrl v Kingdom of Spain, Case No. ARB/14/18 (ICSID May 6, 2022).
Right of Passage over Indian Territory (Portugal v India), ICJ Reports 125 (1957).
Vattenfall AB and Others v Federal Republic of Germany, Case No. ARB/12/12 (ICSID August 31, 2018).

References

Ago, R. (1970). Second report on state responsibility. *II Yearbook of International Law Commission, 2*(177), 192–193.

Avi-Yonah, R. S., & Mazzoni, G. (2018). BEPS, ATAP, and the new tax dialogue: A transatlantic competition? *Intertax, 46*(11), 885.

Beyerlin, U. (2013). Sustainable development. *Max Planck Encyclopaedia of Public International Law, 15.*

Bodansky, D. (1999). *The Framework Convention/Protocol Approach* (No. Paper 1; Technical Briefing Series). World Health Organization (WHO). https://iris.who.int/handle/10665/65355

Bodansky, D., Brunnée, J., & Rajamani, L. (2017). *International climate change law* (p. 121). Oxford University Press.

Brundtland, G. H. (1987). *Our common future: The World Commission on Environment and Development.* Oxford University Press.

CE Delft. (2022). *Maritime shipping and EU ETS: An assessment of the possibilities to evade ETS costs.* Retrieved November 25, 2024, from https://cedelft.eu/publications/maritime-shipping-and-eu-ets-an-assessment-of-the-possibilities-to-evade-ets-costs/

CEDAW. (2016). *Concluding observations on the combined fourth and fifth periodic reports of Switzerland* (No. CEDAW/C/CHE/CO/4-5; p. paras 40–43).

CEDAW. (2018). *Concluding observations on the combined sixth and seventh periodic reports of Luxembourg* (No. CEDAW/C/LUX/CO/6-7; p. paras 10, 15, 16).

Cui, W. (2020). What is unilateralism in international taxation? *AJIL Unbound, 114*, 260.

Dworkin, R. (1977). *Taking rights seriously* (p. 24). Harvard University Press.

Group of Twenty (G20). (2024). *G20 Rio de Janeiro Leaders' Declaration* (p. para 20). Retrieved June 8, 2025, from https://g20.gov.br/en/documents/g20-rio-de-janeiro-leaders-declaration

Handl, G. (1995). Sustainable development: General rules versus specific obligations. In W. Lang (Ed.), *Sustainable development and international law* (p. 35). Graham & Trotman.

Hill, J. (2023). *Aust's modern treaty law and practice* (4th ed.). Cambridge University Press.

International Court of Justice (ICJ). (2025, July 23). *Obligations of States in respect of climate change (ICJ AO).* Retrieved July 27, 2025, from https://www.icj-cij.org/sites/default/files/case-related/187/187-20250723-adv-01-00-en.pdf

International Institute for Sustainable Development (IISD). (n.d.). *Summary report, 3–6 February 2025: Organizational Session for the Intergovernmental Negotiations for the UN Framework Convention on International Tax Cooperation.* Retrieved October 8, 2025, from https://enb.iisd.org/un-framework-convention-international-tax-cooperation-organizational-session-summary

International Law Commission (ILC). (2006a). *Conclusions of the work of the Study Group on the Fragmentation of International Law: Difficulties arising from the Diversification and Expansion of International Law* (No. UN Doc A/61/10).

International Law Commission (ILC). (2006b). *Report of the International Law Commission Fifty-eighth session (1 May-9 June and 3 July-11 August 2006)* (No. UN Doc A/61/10; p. para 251).

International Law Commission (ILC). (2006c). *Report of the International Law Commission Fifty-Eighth Session (1 May–9 June and 3 July–11 August 2006)* (No. UN Doc A/61/10; p. 413). United Nations.

Klabbers, J. (2024). *International law* (4th ed., p. 312). Cambridge University Press (CUP).

McLachlan, C. (2005). The principle of systemic integration and Article 31(3)(c) of the Vienna Convention. *International and Comparative Law Quarterly (ICLQ), 54*, 279, 293.

McLachlan, C. (2024). *The principle of systemic integration in international law*. Oxford University Press.

Neumann, P. (1970). The relationship between GATT and the United Nations. *Cornell International Law Journal, 3*(1), 63–78.

Noonan, C., & Plekhanova, V. (2023). Mandatory binding dispute resolution in the Base Erosion and Profit Shifting (BEPS) two pillar solution. *International and Comparative Law Quarterly, 72*, 437.

OECD. (2013). *Action plan on Base Erosion and Profit Shifting* (pp. 8, 15). Organisation for Economic Cooperation and Development.

OECD. (2017). *Multilateral Convention to Implement Tax Treaty related measures to prevent Base Erosion and Profit Shifting* (No. OECD/LEGAL/0432; p. Article 19). https://www.oecd.org/tax/treaties/multilateral-convention-to-implement-tax-treaty-related-measures-to-prevent-BEPS.htm

OECD. (2024). *Tax and development at the OECD: A retrospective (2009–2024).*

Perrault, C., & Grimm, B. (n.d.). *The classic tale of "Sleeping Beauty."*

Peters, P. (1995). Recent developments in expropriation clauses of Asian Investment Treaties. *Asian Yearbook of International Law, 5*(45), 52.

Picciotto, S. (2017). *The G20 and the Base Erosion and Profit Shifting (BEPS) Project* [Discussion Paper 18/2017]. German Development Institute.

Simma, B. (1994). From bilateralism to community interest in international law. *RdC, 250*, 233.

Tunkin and Waldock. (1964). Summary records of the Sixteenth Session 11 May-24 July 1964. *Yearbook of the International Law Commission, 1*, 310.

United Nations. (1992). *Rio Declaration on Environment and Development* (No. UN Doc A/CONF.151/26). UN Conference on Environment and Development.

United Nations. (2023). *Resolution: 78/459: Macroeconomic policy questions: Promotion of inclusive and effective international cooperation on tax matters at the United Nations: Report of the Second Committee* (No. UN Doc A/78/459/Add.8). United Nations General Assembly, Second Committee.

Inputs to the First Session: United Nations Ad Hoc Committee to Draft Terms of Reference for a United Nations Framework Convention on International Tax Cooperation. https://financing.desa.un.org/un-tax-convention/first-session

Inputs to the Second Session: United Nations Committee to Draft Terms of Reference for a United Nations Framework Convention on International Tax Cooperation. https://financing.desa.un.org/un-tax-convention/second-session

United Nations General Assembly (UNGA). (1990). *Resolution 45/212* (No. UN Doc A/RES/45/212; p. preamble recital 8).

United Nations General Assembly (UNGA). (2023). *Resolution 78/230: Promotion of inclusive and effective International Tax Cooperation at the United Nations* (No. UN Doc A/RES/78/230). United Nations General Assembly.

United Nations General Assembly (UNGA). (2024). *Chair's proposal for draft terms of reference (TOR)* (No. UN Doc A/AC.295/2024/L.4.).

Vella, J. (2025). What is wrong with the international business tax system? *Journal of International Economic Law, 27*(4), 596.

Villiger, M. E. (2009). *Commentary on the 1969 Vienna Convention on the Law of Treaties*. Martinus Nijhoff Publishers.

Vogel, K. (1988). Worldwide vs. Source Taxation of Income – A review and re-evaluation of arguments (Part I). *Intertax, 16*(8), 216.

Wolfrum, R. (2019). Solidarity and community interests: Driving forces for the interpretation and development of international law. *Recueil des Cours, 416*, 163.

Zucman, G. (2024). A blueprint for a coordinated minimum effective taxation standard for ultra-high-net-worth individuals. *EU Tax Observatory*. https://www.taxobservatory.eu/publication/a-blueprint-for-a-coordinated-minimum-effective-taxation-standard-for-ultra-high-net-worth-individuals/

References

[illegible]

Chapter 9
Conclusions

Abstract The FTC proposes a pivotal shift toward inclusive, equitable global tax governance, driven by Global South initiatives, but faces implementation hurdles. Success requires operationalizing principles through additional and new normativity to achieve practical outcomes, leveraging areas of consensus.

The FTC represents a pivotal moment in the evolution of global tax governance, mainly driven by the Global South, proposing an ambitious and necessary advancement of the international tax system. However, as the above analysis highlights, the FTC's path forward is fraught with challenges stemming from persistent North-South tensions, the complexities of operationalizing protocols, and the limitations of its aspirational principles. These dynamics underscore both the opportunities for transformative reform and the hurdles to achieving tangible outcomes.

The North-South divide, evident in the voting patterns of UN resolutions (e.g., Resolution 78/230, with 125 states in favour and 48 opposed) and negotiations at the Ad Hoc Committee and INC, remains a central obstacle. LMICs, led by the African Group, view the FTC as a corrective to the OECD's dominance, which they argue has failed to address their needs, particularly in equitable taxing rights and digital economy challenges. In contrast, HICs advocate for complementarity with existing frameworks like the OECD's IF, preferring consensus-based decision-making to preserve established norms. The hybrid decision-making model adopted in 2025—two-thirds majority for substantive issues, simple majority for procedural matters—reflects a compromise but also the ongoing distrust, exemplified by the United States' withdrawal from discussions. This divide complicates the FTC's ambition to establish a universally accepted framework, yet the incremental shift toward majority voting and the focus on unresolved issues like source taxation on cross-border services suggest a potential for progress, provided practical complementarity with OECD outcomes is maintained.

The FTC's protocols offer a promising avenue to translate principles into binding obligations, targeting areas like tax evasion, IFFs, and environmental taxation, where consensus is less contentious. The prioritization of protocols on cross-border services and dispute resolution reflects a strategic focus on gaps left by OECD-led

E. Vanderbruggen, *Reconstructing Global Tax Governance*, SpringerBriefs in Law, https://doi.org/10.1007/978-981-95-5617-5_9

efforts, such as source taxation and inclusive dispute mechanisms. However, challenges persist, as HICs and LMICs diverge on specifics, such as the scope of source taxation or the acceptance of binding arbitration. The flexibility to define protocol details offers opportunities for tailored measures—e.g., public CbC reporting or taxing ultra-high-net-worth individuals—but requires navigating complementarity with existing frameworks like the Global Forum. The success of these protocols hinges on balancing inclusivity with practicality, ensuring they address Global South priorities without duplicating effective OECD mechanisms.

There is cause for a modicum of optimism. Broad consensus exists on the necessity of international tax cooperation to tackle issues like tax evasion, BEPS, tax competition and digital economy challenges, which unilateral or bilateral approaches cannot effectively address. Both HICs and LMICs recognize the UN's unique institutional role, particularly in areas like international transportation, and agree on high-level principles such as fairness, equity, and alignment with human rights and sustainable development. However, as noted, this consensus often remains abstract, lacking agreement on specific outcomes, as exemplified by differing interpretations and state perspectives of "fairness". This gap underscores the FTC's challenge: translating aspirational principles into concrete, enforceable rules.

The potential for systemic integration of FTC principles into DTAs, via Article 31(3)(c) of the VCLT, offers only a limited pathway to embed sustainable development, fairness, and human rights into the interpretation of substantive DTA provisions, leaving only the amendment of DTAs to foster deeper alignment. Whereas trade- and investment agreements often provide some textual basis to infuse environmental concerns, these are lacking in DTAs, and some of their more unambiguous clauses (e.g., withholding tax rates) leave little room for extraneous norms unless explicitly referenced. This limitation highlights the FTC's aspirational ambition: principles alone cannot displace existing tax rules without additional normativity to operationalize them.

Ultimately, the FTC's potentially greatest strength—its invocation of core principles to reframe taxation as integral to global goals like sustainable development and human rights—is also its principal limitation. The absence of universal consensus on practical outcomes, as seen in the Ad Hoc Committee's debates, risks leaving the FTC mired in abstract rhetoric. To realize its transformative potential, the FTC must prioritize targeted measures, such as protocols addressing the design and administration of inadequate national tax systems, tax-gaps and novel internationally coordinated tax instruments, to bridge the gap between high-level principles and tangible results. While the commendable initiative of the FTC proposes a significant departure from the bilateral, voluntarist legacies of the international tax system, its success depends on overcoming North-South divides, leveraging areas of consensus, and ensuring that principles like equity and sustainable development translate into practical reforms.

MIX
Papier aus verantwortungsvollen Quellen
Paper from responsible sources
FSC® C105338

If you have any concerns about our products,
you can contact us on
ProductSafety@springernature.com

In case Publisher is established outside the EU,
the EU authorized representative is:
Springer Nature Customer Service Center GmbH
Europaplatz 3, 69115 Heidelberg, Germany

Printed by Libri Plureos GmbH
in Hamburg, Germany